# Liberty and Security

# Liberty and Security

## Conor Gearty

polity

First published in 2013 by Polity Press

Polity Press
65 Bridge Street
Cambridge CB2 1UR, UK

Polity Press
350 Main Street
Malden, MA 02148, USA

ISBN-13: 978-0-7456-4718-0 (hardback)
ISBN-13: 978-0-7456-4719-7 (paperback)

A catalogue record for this book is available from the British Library.

Typeset in 11 on 13 pt Sabon
by Toppan Best-set Premedia Limited
Printed and bound in Great Britain by MPG Books Group Limited, Bodmin, Cornwall

For further information on Polity, visit our website:
www.politybooks.com

# Contents

*Acknowledgements*                                    vi

1 Introduction                                         1
2 Struggling Towards the Universal                     7
3 The Global Stage                                    30
4 The Enemy Within                                    50
5 A Very Partial Freedom                              72
6 Cultural War                                        95
7 Returning to Universals                            108

*Notes*                                              117
*Index*                                              139

# Acknowledgements

This book began life as a couple of talks at my workplace, the London School of Economics, and also at the School of Oriental and African Studies. I am grateful to colleagues who came along for their very helpful input into the ideas that I developed there and which have now grown into this book. In particular, I'd like to thank Alasdair Cochrane, Phil Cook, Neil Duxbury, Steve Hopgood, Paul Kelly, Chandran Kukathas, Annabel Lever, Emmanuel Melissaris, Tom Poole, Peter Ramsay, Mike Redmayne, and Leslie Vinjamuri for their insightful comments and general support. Later on I was very grateful to Aoife Nolan for reading pretty well the whole manuscript and making many helpful suggestions. The book is dedicated to my two lovely children, now pretty well grown up, Eliza and Owen.

# 1

# Introduction

What do we mean when we use the terms 'liberty' and 'security'? The first has a range which takes it across a spectrum, from the essence of human freedom at one end, to a far narrower statement about the need for unrestrained movement at the other. Liberty is sometimes thought of as concerned with the individual *qua* individual. On other occasions, it is presented as the individual *within* society. At one moment the word seems to be about the need to be left alone by all authority, while at the next, it positively suggests active participation in the government of the state. No one seems quite sure whether 'liberty' is – in any of its incarnations – the same as 'civil liberties', and even if it is, there are, as Jeremy Waldron has pointed out, at least four separate meanings to the latter term.[1] As for the lawyers, in pre-rights days they got into the habit of thinking of 'civil liberties' as primarily concerned with the law on the control of police powers, and this is a space that the subject still occupies in practice, in the UK at least and sometimes further afield as well.[2]

The term 'security' has a similar range and equivalent levels of vagueness. Used in conjunction with liberty, security has historically been taken to refer to 'national' security, to the protection from external and perhaps even internal threat of particular lands organized as states.[3] The field of

*Introduction*

counter-terrorism has grown out of this orientation of security towards territorial protection. Taking a different tack, we now also see the idea of security being reconfigured for the global age as 'human security' – an approach to protection that focuses on people, not places, and which tries to get beyond immediate attacks on freedom to systemic failures in the public sphere that render us all (in a broader sense) less secure.[4] Lurking in the background is the idea of security as a guarantor of well being, captured in a contemporary term, 'social security', now so familiar to us that we have forgotten the startling idealism and ambition that once oozed from these two words.[5]

Paradoxically this uncertainty over the meaning of 'liberty' and 'security' has not detracted from their power as positive signifiers within many contemporary discourses, societal, political and legal. The first suggests freedom, an unconstrained self, a life lived to its full, flourishing limit. The second secures the space for such a life, hedging it against the threats that might destroy it, seeing off the intrusions that threaten to make this success impossible. In this way, security is the platform for liberty, simultaneously constituting a launching pad and safe landing place for the soaring self. These words echo across the European languages ('liberté'; 'libertas'; 'sécurité'; 'securitas') but also find expression in other tongues with different etymological roots: the practical impact of these phrases may be confusing but the thought behind them (the free person safe from harm) is universal.

This book is about the shape that these words have taken through time and from place to place, how much they have been realized and for how many, and what their standing is today. What mainly occupies us here is not their core meaning so much as it is the reach of the benefits that each so powerfully evokes. It is the 'for how many' issue that mainly concerns us: to whom are liberty and security to be extended? Is it to be to all or just the few? If it is to be to all, is it to be through community, state, non-state, regional or international action? If guaranteed for all, how practical in their reach do these theoretical commitments prove themselves to be, or – to put this in a cruder way – for all the fine talk, what is *truly* going on *on the ground*?

The central arguments over liberty and security have really always been about this issue of remit rather than of meaning. They are reflected in the growing presence of walls in divided societies, blatant efforts by the 'haves' to shut out not only the sight of the 'have-nots' but also any opportunity the unlucky many might have to glimpse what a better future would look like. Israel's 'partition fence' might be the most well known of these but it is by no means the only one.[6]

To ask if liberty is constituted by 'freedom from' external constraint rather than 'freedom to' access the necessities for a good life is immediately to raise this question of whose freedom we have in mind. Our answer will reveal whether we are thinking of those already in a position to live a decent life (and who want to protect it) or those for whom presently it is a faraway dream. Equally when we talk of 'personal security' or 'national security' or 'human security' or (even) 'social security', it is immediately clear that our differences with each other will be mainly about who is to enjoy these valuable protections, rather than what it means to be safeguarded in these various ways.

This book tracks the breadth of these terms, tracing the fluctuating range of beneficiaries to be found within their remit. It argues as well for a particular approach, one that regards the benefits of liberty and security as being rightfully available to all, and thereby capable of reaching (being required to reach) the many rather than the few. The book does not argue the ethic of such a perspective from first principles. Instead it rather takes the moral desirability of universality for granted – as most societies now say they do (whatever about how they truly act). Viewing liberty and security in this all-inclusive way shapes how I approach both the past work these words have done and the present-day reach that (I say) should be consistently accorded to them.

This is not as easy as it might seem. If we look beyond the present, neither term has been routinely understood in

such broad terms; indeed (as we shall see) the primary understanding of liberty and security in the pre-democratic era was
always narrowly selective as to who was to benefit from the
opportunities afforded the one and the safety delivered by
the other. It was only when the radically egalitarian idea of
community self-government took hold on a national scale
that liberty and security found themselves open to being
wrenched out of their elitist corrals and offered to all.
Democracy gave the universalist reading of liberty and security an entry point and strong support, but it could not by
itself deliver effortless supremacy for the reach that this
approach affords these words. This was because (as we shall
see shortly) the democratic victory was itself incomplete, a
freedom for all that was invariably not forged afresh but
rather tentatively grafted onto a pre-existing society that had
been designed for the few. Old elite readings of liberty and
security persisted into the democratic era, jostling for space
with their egalitarian interlopers.

And now, as we drift towards a post-democratic model
of government (or as I will be calling it here 'neo-democratic'), a polity that increasingly wears democratic clothes
as a disguise rather than a proud necessity, we see these old
pre-democratic meanings of the terms returning into popular
use, underpinning and explaining readings of liberty and
security, which remain ostentatiously universal but are now
falsely so – words that hide inequality and unfairness by
seeming to reach all when in fact in their practical impact
they are tailored to the few. It is this sense of double standards, of saying something and acting in a way that is quite
different, that underpins the ethic of universalism which
drives forward the central argument of this book.

Risking repetition, let me put this in another way, since
it maps out so much of what is to follow. I am not interested
here in precise definition so much as I am in reach. My thesis
is that we need to recover and re-energize true universalism
in the way that we use these terms 'liberty' and 'security'.
Here are two words that grew to prominence at a time when
the work they did was at the service of the few but which,

under the energetic influence of the democratic impulse, became the goals towards which it was right for government to work on behalf of all. Now this expansionist trend is being halted by a drift away from democratic fundamentals and back towards elite readings of liberty and security, albeit these versions remain cloaked in apparently universalist language, an echo of past, more egalitarian times. My contention here is that we need to grab back and restore these democratic readings before (I am tempted to add) it is too late and we have forgotten what it means for everybody to enjoy these great life-chances, not only to imagine what is behind the wall, but to walk through to that better life as well.

The version of liberty and security that I argue for here has three important allies in its quest to impose its version of the truth; large-scale movements that have had a beneficial impact across the world. These are (as we have already seen) the move towards democratic government, and also the rule of law and respect for human rights. The first is clearly the main driver behind the insistence that the privileges of the few should be made available to the many. The second predates the democratic turn but complements it, maintaining that everyone must be subject to the same laws and (just as critically) that the maker of any given law should not at one and the same time be its authoritative interpreter. The third, the human rights movement, is of more recent origin (at least insofar as we understand the idea today); the very way that its self-description dedicates itself to all humans reveals the commitment shown by human rights to an egalitarian vision of the world, one in which we all should have a right to the freedoms that were once assumed to be the privilege of the few. And human rights today also reach beyond the protection of liberty (narrowly defined) to encompass rich readings of human security, the sort to which I alluded a moment ago and which democratic government once made popular.

The neo-democratic turn wants us to regard democracy, the rule of law and human rights as outmoded. It wants us to see these ideas as 'old hat', incapable of coping with the challenges of the modern global world, the rise of extremism, climate change, the movement of capital, population growth, refugees, etc. Now perhaps (as will sometimes be suggested in the chapters that follow) there is a link between the current supremacy of the market (hiding under the pseudo-scientific 'neo-liberal' label) and the neo-democracy that I am describing. The connection strikes me as present but it is not a necessary link in my argument. Whatever their underlying perspective, the proponents of neo-democracy (conscious and unconscious) are happy to see the terms 'liberty' and 'security' contaminated by misuse, forsaken by those who should love them most as creatures of illusion and hypocrisy. True liberty and security – that is liberty and security for all and not just the already empowered few – depends on recovering the finest meanings of these terms and then using them as offensive weapons against the onward surge of the over-privileged minority whose ideal world would see liberty and security as their exclusive preserve alone. They must be resisted.

# 2

# Struggling Towards the Universal

## Liberty Captured by Security

Of course it is possible to go back to antiquity in our search for the origins of the idea of liberty. Like Benjamin Constant we could start with the Greeks, as in his justly famed lecture in 1819, *The Liberty of the Ancients Compared with that of the Moderns*.[1] Or we could dive into the world of Niccolò Machiavelli, a writer who 'uses "liberty" in a bewildering variety of senses' the effect of which is to make it very hard 'to pin down his idea with any precision'.[2] When discussing such perennially important terms there will always be an element of arbitrariness to whatever is the chosen starting point. I am beginning here by making a journey back into the 1640s, to the turmoil of the English civil wars from which so much of our contemporary understanding of liberty and security has flowed, not only in Britain and the US but around the world as well. The various threads to their meaning that emerged then endure today, strongly influencing the question of remit upon which, as I have said in the introduction, I mainly want to focus.

During these vital years, a brilliant apologist for English royal power grabbed hold of the idea of 'liberty' – which was then the most progressive term in the vocabulary of the radicals of the day – and, by dint of a phoney divide with

'security', turned it from an engine of freedom into a rationale for servitude. Thomas Hobbes may not have been the
first servant of power to distort progressive terms to suit his
masters, and as we shall see in the course of this book he
was by no means the last. But he is the most important, with
an influence that as we say these days has 'gone global'. So
this enquiry must start with the Latimer school's star pupil,
later one of Oxford's most famous graduates, and in early
adulthood, a man who earned his bread as the sometimes
teacher and afterwards general intellectual factotum of the
second Earl of Devonshire.[3]

In his first major work, *Elements of Law*,[4] Thomas
Hobbes saw liberty in fairly simplistic terms as a capacity
to act or to forbear from acting, which capacity leads naturally to deliberation as between rival paths (should I go with
my appetites or let my fears triumph?), which in turn pro-
duces a decision, the will to act or not to act as the case
may be. What is marvellous about this, and for its day,
highly original, is how it relegates reason to a sideshow to
the main event, which is all about emotions – feelings,
wants, aversions, and so on. In this world of 'blameless
liberty', we naturally desire what is good for us and seek to
avoid what is bad for us: and above all for Hobbes, this
entails fleeing from death. As Quentin Skinner puts it in his
book *Hobbes and Republican Liberty*, it was for Hobbes
obvious that '[w]e have a natural tendency . . . to do everything we can to preserve our lives'.[5] Because this disposition
is so very reasonable, we must furthermore have the natural
right to act to preserve ourselves *at all costs*. The last phrase
is of course the rub: there is not enough of the world to go
round, and there are too many of us all exercising our
natural right to do whatever we want at the same time, for
us all to be able to be simultaneously satisfied. Consequently,
in Hobbes's famous phrase, the life of man is 'solitary, poor,
nasty, brutish, and short.'[6] To quote Skinner again, '[t]he
desperate paradox on which Hobbes's political theory is
grounded is that the greatest enemy of human nature is
human nature itself.'[7]

The way out of this conundrum lies in obliging ourselves to forbear from acting according to our will and power. This requires submission to a sovereign to whom we are henceforth to be 'as absolutely subject . . . as is a child to the father, or a slave to the master in the state of nature'.[8] Because liberty is impossible, our submission to the protective force of the sovereign is practically absolute: true, Hobbes does have some sense of inalienable rights, but these do not figure prominently in his thinking, and he never seriously contemplated any kind of right of revolution against an iniquitous sovereign. His description of his later book *Leviathan*[9] as 'a work that now fights on behalf of all kings and all who, under whatever name, hold regal rights'[10] stands as a description of the author as well as of much of his output.

Hobbes completed *Elements* in 1640, after which his anthem to sovereign power was rather undermined by facts on the ground, with the then English king Charles I being drawn into an escalating political, and then military, confrontation with Parliament. At the first hint of such trouble, in November 1640, Hobbes bolted. His destination was the France of Cardinal Richelieu and the Bourbon throne – where his comforting views were no doubt regarded as more than making up for his non-Catholicity. As the 1640s progressed, it became increasingly obvious that Hobbes's version of liberty was falling entirely out of kilter with the republican ideals of the progressive forces that were pushing their way to power in England.

This is the alternative story about liberty and security, anticipated in the Introduction, which I need to draw in from the margins of its day and hold at the centre of my narrative for a moment. On this account, liberty was tied up not with what you were able or not able to do, but with the sort of society in which you lived: if the governing regime was despotic, you were unfree, and this was the case, however unimpeded you were so far as day-to-day movement was concerned. Liberty was about living in a free state; without such freedom, the practice of your conduct was bound to be so cautious and so dependent on the power of others, as to be effectively a life of servitude. The most famous example of this aspect of seventeenth-century English radicalism were the Levellers, 'a disciplined political group that came into being no earlier than 1646' albeit '[w]ithin three years, they were a spent force'.[11] Their manifesto of 7 July 1646 *A Remonstrance of many thousand citizens . . .*[12] 'defended the basic liberties of the people including freedom of the press and freedom from impressment into military service'[13] and attacked the laws under which they then laboured as 'unworthy a free people'.[14] The Levellers produced, on 29 October 1647, *An Agreement of the People*, 'a landmark in constitutional history',[15] which apart from setting out the rudiments of 'a system of representative, responsible, accountable, and democratic government'[16] demanded also that 'laws ought to be equal, so they must be good, and not evidently destructive to the safety and well being of the people'.[17] In this last phrase you have in a nutshell what I am arguing for in this book, a vision of security ('safety') and liberty ('well being') which is for all ('the people').

From his secure base abroad, Hobbes took these kinds of Republican views on directly, first in *De Cive*[18] and then most famously of all in *Leviathan*. Far from everything depending on how a country was governed, a 'free-man is he, that in those things, which by his strength and wit he is able to do, is not hindered to do what he has a will to do'.[19] If I choose not to do something merely because I dread the consequences, this does not mean that I am not free to do it; it merely means I do not want to, that is, I am still free. Hobbes defines external impediments very narrowly, therefore broadening the range of freedom – we are free even if we live in a despotic country, cannot afford to eat, and feel we have to comply with damaging laws for fear of vicious punishment.

This version of individual liberty fitted well with Hobbes's grand scheme of liberty-disavowal, developed in *Elements* and re-stated in his later work, because it is largely residual. The few inalienable rights apart (on which, as noted above, Hobbes is not very clear in any event), we are free only insofar as we are not stopped from doing something, and the sovereign's judgment as to when and who to stop can never be contradicted. In particular, what the sovereign does in the name of security goes, and goes without saying, so if it requires that a person be impeded by the force of the state's jailors, then that is simply that – and if he (or she) obeys the law merely because of a wish to avoid this unpleasant eventuality, then such a person remains free even then, for (as just mentioned) choosing to obey a law does not count as an external impediment to liberty.

Of course, merely to state Hobbes's theory in the bald way I have just done is to seem to underline the depth of his defeat as an important and influential thinker, at least so far as his role as an apologist for authoritarianism is concerned. The collapse of the royal forces of Charles I, followed shortly afterwards by the failure of the Commonwealth that succeeded him, led to a move to the 'balanced constitution' of Charles II, which from 1660, quite explicitly resiled from the absolutism of predecessor regimes. After 1688, increasingly the idea of representative government was to take hold, with the democratization process from 1688 to 1948 gradually turning what had by now become the United Kingdom into a republic in substance if not in form. Accompanying this democratization was a large-scale movement to universal liberty as well.

And of course these developments were not unique to England/Britain, though this state was the one that was to foreshadow so much elsewhere. From the nineteenth century on, all the developed nations experienced the same push towards ever-widening franchises with first working men and then both men and women securing an entitlement that only a few generations before would have been incomprehensible to informed opinion. The defeated Axis nations and the colonial states were to follow in the second half of the following century and after 1989 much of the post-Soviet world as well. By the start of the third millennium, therefore, this republican version of freedom – living in a free state – gave every appearance of having been apotheosized into a universal right to democratic government, indeed some human rights specialists even talked in these terms.[20]

With this shift to popular government has come a new sense of 'security', one (anticipated in our Introduction) which has combined resistance to external threats with a new solicitude for the people. Broad readings of security have come into play, echoes of what the Levellers had been thinking about when calling for laws better focused on the 'safety' and 'well being' of the people. Starting in Bismarck's Germany in the nineteenth century, and gradually spreading to the rest of the emerging democratic world, the idea of security as a protection for all within a state gradually took hold. The United Kingdom had its own particular contribution in the form of first the 1909 minority report by Beatrice and Sydney Webb into the iniquities of the then well-entrenched poor law system[21] and subsequently in the actions of later Liberal and particularly Labour administrations. The description of a 'welfare' (as opposed to 'warfare') state appears first to have been used by Archbishop William Temple during the Second World War.[22] At the same time, in the United States, President Roosevelt was reconfiguring the idea of freedom to include not only 'freedom from fear' but also 'freedom from want', by which the president meant 'economic understandings which will secure to every nation a healthy peacetime life for its inhabitants'.[23] In the post-war world of civil and political, but also economic, social, and cultural human rights, it was certainly not Hobbes's vision which appeared to have triumphed, but that of the Levellers – 'rebels of the present time' as Hobbes had called them.[24]

## Escaping Hobbes?

The form of government prevailing today tells us that we now live in a world framed by a largely democratic environment that prizes liberty and security for all. And yet it is clear that the ostensibly democratic shape our society takes does not tell the full story of the present moment, one in which vast disparities of wealth persist both across and within states, in which a great many lead unfulfilled lives of difficult precariousness, a time in which in the language of this book neither 'liberty' nor 'security' is available in any kind of tangible way to many. It is extraordinary how much inequality and injustice has persisted into the democratic era, in some countries just as bad as in previous times, in a few desperately unlucky regions even worse.[25] Democracy and human rights abound almost as much as the poverty that their presence appears to have done so little to prevent.

Skinner ends his study by admitting that in Hobbes's 'assault on the republican theory of liberty . . . we can hardly fail to acknowledge that he won the battle'.[26] While this may be perhaps overstating things a little, there is no doubt that Hobbes remains hugely influential, not least in the way in which his early contamination of the liberty-security discourse damaged progress towards democracy from the outset and so helped make possible the neo-democratic turn which I mentioned earlier and to which I return later in this chapter. How can the facts of the current times be so much at odds with the outcomes that are supposed to be delivered by the democratic government whose job it is to stand vigilant guard over the interests of the many? How can we have ended up where we are, with a world that is seemingly shaped by the standards of democracy, the rule of law and human rights but which delivers so little liberty and security to those whose lives are supposed to be emancipated by the practical operation of these liberating slogans?

The first point to make by way of an answer is not directly connected to Hobbes: it is to notice how in Britain, and indeed (at least as importantly for this book) later everywhere else, the republican triumph has been less complete than the universal democratic narrative just outlined would have us suppose. This is not entirely about form, though of course the United Kingdom (in common with other democracies) does remain distinctly non-republican in its retention of the monarchy. At least some other seemingly republican states find themselves applauding by their vote members of the families of earlier elected rulers (for instance, President George W. Bush and Prime Minister Lee Kuan Yew in Singapore). The main point however is that though the vote has been conceded, and participation in the election of the governors of the state guaranteed to all but the entirely incompetent,[27] this has not produced the renaissance of the free-born citizen that many proponents of the vote (nostalgic for a magically unlived past in antiquity perhaps) may have assumed would inevitably follow.

The evidence for the imperfect success of the republican/democratic impulse, the weaknesses that have flowed from its having been merely tentatively grafted on to an earlier unjust status quo, can be seen all around us, in the power of private money, the systemic defects in prevailing constitutional orders, the lure of populist nationalism, the temptation to indulge in a rhetoric of fear, and the lack of energetic engagement in self-governance revealed by many citizens. These have all combined, with other factors no doubt (such as the conservative tendencies of state bureaucracies), to debilitate the operation in practice of the republican/democratic form of government. The result is that our republican freedom remains under-expressed in democratic society, and even when it emerges, its flourishing is often stunted by anxiety.

This situation has been compounded by the tensions generated by the fear of external attack and internal subversion that was such a dominant aspect of the democratic polity right from its first successes at the end of the nineteenth century through to the collapse of the Berlin Wall (and with it socialist confidence) in 1989. And even before the assaults of 11 September 2001 (on which, of course, more presently) there have been the challenges of multiculturalism and of politically motivated subversive violence, or 'terrorism' as it is invariably called, each of which would have tested the mettle of even an ideally functioning republican state. When we add to all this the pressures on states derived from the asymmetry of the power of nations across the world, and the consequent vulnerability of fragile states to the interests of the powerful, our dreadful colonial legacy, it is sometimes surprising that so much functioning democracy remains in the world rather than that there is so little.

A second aspect to the imperfect triumph of republican ideas also focuses less on Hobbes and more on the sort of republican victory that was achieved in the generations after the English revolution of the seventeenth century, both in Britain and in later years (as democratic forms of government spread) further afield. This relates to a failure on the part of republicanism to think through properly what individual liberty in a free state entails as a matter of *personal* (as opposed to *societal*) freedom: it is all very well to live in a free society but what does that mean for me, am I bound to be a free person simply because I am within this free state? When republicanism was only an ideal for elites, as it was in its post-Leveller but triumphant early days (1688 in England; 1776 in what became the United States of America), it was easy for proponents of this form of government to assume that a free society meant freedom for each and all – they could make this move because they were simply leaving most of the population out of their account, the invisible women and working poor and (in some cases) native peoples who were not to have any part in this unfolding drama of freedom.

The reshaping of republicanism as democracy from the nineteenth century onwards broke this link between individual and collective freedom, and indeed threatened the liberties of the elite few with the new and now realistic demands for liberty and security for the many. It is absolutely right to say that this push for universalism achieved a great deal in terms of improving the life chances and security of the population as a whole – I have already mentioned the growth of the ideas of universal welfare and human rights. But this was achieved in a way which never successfully challenged the prevailing power relations within democratic society, power relations which were (as we have just seen) themselves a hangover from the imperfect transition from despotism to democracy via elite republicanism. The rich conceded liberty and security for all as long as they could stay rich (or relatively rich) – equality was henceforth to be about opportunity not possessions. Everybody could play the game of life but no one was to be allowed to mention how tilted was the playing field.

This is an important point for my overall argument. The idea that equality meant that you were to have a chance equal to everybody else to grow your liberty in the context of a security equally available to all gave way to an illusory equality, one in which the poor and those just above this level were required to believe that they had the same depth of opportunity as the rich. Of course putting it like this is clearly to reveal it as an exaggeration: democracy has always had its radical socialist and egalitarian detractors as well as its liberal defenders. But crucially all these critics have conceded the imperative of working for change from *within* rather than *in opposition* to existing structures. The Fabian socialists of early twentieth-century Britain may have been something of a caricature in their fetishizing of a Roman general famous for doing nothing at all, but they capture something of a truth about permissible radical discourse in our imperfect democratic era.

For those prepared to go further, liberty and security have always quickly evaporated in practice. Here now is the consequence of this second aspect of the imperfect republican triumph anticipated a moment ago. So far as these radical critics of the democratic state were concerned, those prepared to bring the whole edifice down and build something new, republican thought was practically Hobbesian in the blank cheque it gives to authority, albeit now a different kind of authority, republican rather than despotic. This aggressive element to republicanism pre-dates democracy, with even that great republican figure John Milton having been unabashed in his willingness to act against Catholics, and also (more seriously from the perspective of this book) perfectly happy to clamp down on sedition (while of course, it is acknowledged, objecting to controls on publication in advance).[28] But it came into its stride in the fierce opposition displayed by democratic/republican states everywhere to radical challenges to their authority, producing a series of harsh assaults on the individual freedom of 'subversives' within the state that have not been at odds with republican readings of liberty and security so much as positively justified by them.

Mainly this has been about controlling anti-war activities and Communist speech, the kind of people prepared to challenge from the Left the very organizational principles upon which the new democratic deal had been done.[29] Thus in one English case during the First World War, Mr Justice Darling explicitly interpreted a challenged regulation in accordance with the maxim *salus populi suprema lex*.[30] Courts were so keen to support the conduct of war by democratic government that they were justifiably accused by one exasperated (and dissenting) judge of being 'more executive minded than the executive'.[31] Communists and other socialist radicals fared badly wherever in the democratic world they happened to find themselves, their meetings interrupted by police,[32] their public demonstrations disrupted[33] and on occasion their political parties simply banned.[34] Nor did supposed constitutional protection for free speech for such activists make any difference, as opponents of the United States's system of government found to their cost in a series of Supreme Court decisions squaring attacks on their liberty with ostensibly unqualified guarantees of free speech.[35] When one British Home Secretary defended himself against charges of the partisan use of the law against Communists, he explained that the people concerned were outside the law which was concerned only with defending 'the right type of freedom of speech'.[36]

## Managing Dysfunction

How could such a mismatch between the theory of universal liberty and its obviously selective practice have gone so largely unchallenged in democratic society? At one level the answer lies in something I alluded to a moment ago, the way in which democratic society has invariably been constructed, as a kind of compromise between power and the people – this has to entail (if the people are to keep their side of the bargain) that radical and/or revolutionary change is rendered difficult if not impossible. But it goes further than this, into the deep structure of what we understand liberty to mean, and in examining this we find Hobbes returning and his global legacy at its most influential.

This takes us to the rule of law. Now I have already mentioned the power of this idea as a proponent of the kind of universalist reading of liberty which I am proposing here, and I have no desire to argue against this as a general principle. The value of a commitment to legality even in an undemocratic or merely partly democratic society is that the officers of such a state have then to justify themselves by reference to something other than their own or their master's whim. An example is the famous decision of *Entick v Carrington*,[37] in the pre-democratic Britain of 1765, in which the chief justice Lord Camden led his fellow judges in denying government the power to act as it wished against a political opponent on an asserted principle of 'state necessity'. That court's condemnation of impugned government action as unlawful because ungrounded in law has informed later generations of civil libertarian defence against executive excess, and helps to explain why even such a distinguished radical historian as E. P. Thompson should have characterized the rule of law as (in his famous phrase) 'an unqualified good'.[38]

But look again at *Entick v Carrington*. While the basis for the denial of the power that was sought to be exercised – a right of entry and seizure of papers – was the continuing right to property enjoyed by John Entick (expressed in terms redolent of John Locke as 'the great end for which men entered into society' having been 'to secure their property'), this was not an absolute right, but was rather one 'which is preserved sacred and incommunicable in all instances *where it has not been taken away or abridged* by some public law for the good of the whole'.[39] Thus in proper Hobbesian fashion, the right to property did not precede law; though expressed in the judgment in positive terms, it was in fact residual. The issue in the case was not the invasion of the right to property as such; rather it was the absence of a legal basis for the infringement. *Leviathan* had not spoken properly, that was all.

As this case illustrates, Hobbes's residual theory of liberty had already taken a firm grip of British law in the mid eighteenth century and it continued to have immense influence in the decades, even centuries, that followed and therefore, through British influence, on other legal systems as well. Promoted in particular by the Oxford professor Albert Venn Dicey in the nineteenth century,[40] this residual account of liberty (backed by remedies where the freedom is unlawfully transgressed) bedded down so successfully in England that it is only now, and very slowly, being eroded by the move to rights. In the US likewise, so robust has the idea of innate freedom proved to be that 'libertarianism' has not only avoided submergence in the constitutional rights culture of the founding fathers but has managed to re-emerge in recent years as one of the key obstacles to governmental action for anything other than the defence of the state itself from external attack (taking the shape of what is often called 'libertarianism').

This all fits very neatly with Hobbes. As we saw earlier, his theory requires that liberty be both extensive (in this residual sense of being the presumptive position) and at the same time vulnerable to aggressive state action, capable of being smashed if *Leviathan* judges such repressive action to be essential to the safety of the state. Now it is perfectly possible in theory for a democratic state to throw up challenges to power emanating from those who are less advantaged than are the powerful and to whom the right to vote has given articulate leaders. The transition to democracy produced many such moments, such as (in Britain) the agitation for an extended franchise and in Europe generally in 1848. Nor has the move made by proto-democracies to a welfare state model always been easy: aristocratic resistance to Lloyd George's 'People's Budget' of 1909 being a well-known case in point from the UK. With democracy has certainly come the occasional egalitarian assault on power and privilege which, by threatening to break the grand bargain between the people and power, has provoked a strongly negative reaction from the rich, over high taxation for example or a government's policy of nationalization. Democracy may not be a total radical success – but nor has it been an absolute failure: some structures have been shaken, others brought down, new more egalitarian frameworks erected in their place.

Things have, however, changed since these periods of democratic turmoil. Such moments of serious concern for the wealthy as attended the birth-pangs of democracy were always rare and now they are almost non-existent. (Rages against neo-liberalism on the street are not usually dangerous to power and often have too much of an anarchic quality to go anywhere other than a police cell.)[41] The result of the imperfect realization of the democratic value of equality, therefore, is that those with fortuitously disproportionate access to wealth today find that they need to challenge the state very little while being able happily to use their liberty to lead life to the full. Their freedom is all the freer for the fact that they need never seriously question the world in which they (through the accident of birth or class) find themselves. This is true of the very rich but it is equally the case with the merely affluent, in other words those who are advantaged by their situation in life compared to many, and whose relatively fortunate situation means that they are not disposed to worry about those top-end disparities which in fact show them as comparatively less well off.

But it is different for those on the outside trying to force their way in, or to challenge the half-hearted nature of the democratic settlement in any kind of serious, radical way: the jibe in the last paragraph about street protest leading to the police cell was meant seriously. We saw this when we discussed the case law justifying state action against subversives a moment ago and now we need to link this point to the underlying theory, to see how it can be made to make sense in terms of what liberty entails. When Dicey wrote confidently about there being no rights in the English system at all, but rather a series of freedoms that existed because all were free unless the state (whether under statute or the common law) had acted to control their liberty,[42] he was making an assumption about non-intervention which may have been true of him and his milieu, but which was distinctly untrue about whole categories of persons (trade unionists; socialists; women in search of the vote; Irish nationalists) of whom Dicey either knew very little or whose causes he deplored.[43] The pattern set in the last decades of the nineteenth century subsisted until right through to the end of the twentieth. The point extends beyond Dicey, beyond Britain. For the bulk of the population, freedom was evident in the ease with which they went about their daily lives: there was no difference between the quality of the various kinds of acts that an individual desired to do – it might be shopping, sight-seeing, or queuing for theatre tickets – or (and of course very few of them did this) it might be attending a political meeting with a view to seeking a particular reform, or engaging in a mass demonstration. The law did not distinguish between any of these, much less attach greater importance to the political over the apolitical – and the great majority of the people in a democracy are invariably wedded to the apolitical. Though all were in theory equally vulnerable to the intervention of *Leviathan* (expressed either through statute or via the common/judge-made law), in practice, only those who challenged power were made the victims of state coercion.

With this set of observations, we come to the central point about Hobbes's enduring influence on our understanding of what liberty and security entail. As we have seen his key idea involves an outlandishly extreme commitment to individual freedom combined with a deep precariousness so far as the protection of that liberty is concerned. Now, this balance between freedom and insecurity is only unsatisfactory if you experience the wide freedom it gives you as precarious, if the contingent nature of the exercise of your liberty is before you all the time. If it is not, if *Leviathan* rarely intrudes on you, your family, or your immediate community (in other words the people you know) then the fragility inherent in your liberty is not to the foreground of your thinking. It is the freedom you experience, not the ease with which it is taken away. The latter may be something that others suffer – alleged revolutionaries; suspected 'terrorists'; fifth-columnists; indigenous rights activists; foreigners who seek to subvert the state from within – but because they are not you or like you, and of course you never meet them, their vulnerability does not register.

In designing a system which turns everything over to *Leviathan*, while assuring the majority that *Leviathan* will not challenge their freedom to pursue their individual appetites as they wish as long as they do not rock the boat, Hobbes produced an artifice which has remained attractive long after the monarchs and despots for whom he argued have been slung from centre stage. It has endured right into the democratic era, a time when servitude may have disappeared, but a recognizably Hobbesian apolitical, selfish passivity (the pursuit of individualist desires) has, if anything, – fuelled by its compatibility with capitalist modes of thought – come even further into prominence. In the democratic era we see an imperfect self-government with a rule of law willing to accommodate Republican state action of a Leviathan nature, and as a result producing a partial remit for liberty and security. The system is exemplified in those occasional crises where the wrong person (a white suspected arms-dealer; a crooked but conventional banker; a media tycoon facing criminal charges) finds him- or herself falling foul of the law: the majoritarian stampede for fair play then is almost wondrous to behold: 'that law is not for *us*' you can almost hear them say.

## Imperfect Protectors

But what of human rights, with democracy and the rule of law our third bridge from the particular to our desired, universalist reading of liberty and security? Has it also its faults, eroding its universalism in the way that echoes the damage done to both democracy and the rule of law? The Levellers had spoken of 'the basic liberties of the people' and during the Second World War President Franklin Roosevelt had asserted his four freedoms, which had included (as we have seen) 'freedom from fear' and 'freedom from want'. After the war, as also briefly mentioned earlier, this kind of political language took a fresh shape in a new human rights vocabulary. From the outset, international human rights law was about liberty in the broad sense and also the kind of security that would be necessary to make that liberty real. The Universal Declaration of Human Rights talked of civil and political freedom but also about the need for work, pay, rest, leisure, a home, health-care and (understandably given earlier Nazi assaults on learning) a right to participate in the cultural life of the community. This declaration was then (albeit slowly) worked up into two international agreements, covering respectively economic, social and cultural rights[44] and civil and political rights.[45] In the immediate aftermath of the war, similar initiatives took place at the regional level (the European Convention on Human Rights; the American Declaration of the Rights and Duties of Man) and in the Axis states where democratic governing systems were being newly established in the aftermath of defeat. The spread of democratic forms of government in post-colonial and, more recently, in post-Soviet states has also invariably involved a move towards this wide reading of human rights, and often they are justiciable in the courts as well.

There can be little doubt that the institutionalization of human rights in international relations and in law that we have seen in the sixty-five years since the Universal Declaration has done no little good, providing a legal basis for the rich reading of liberty and security argued for here. A key feature of all of these rights advances has been a prohibition on discrimination, with the universalist leanings of the language of human rights being most evident in this determination to break the assumption that some (the citizens; the rich;

the male) are to be treated inherently more favourably than others. It has provided a framework for a critique of states whose ill-treatment of their own citizens would otherwise have been able to shelter under the protection afforded by the respect for state sovereignty (regardless of their political character) that is the other main feature of the post-war settlement. The (admittedly uneven) availability of judicial mechanisms of accountability has also sometimes severely embarrassed colonial powers in the exercise of their extra-territorial powers.[46] In the domestic context, human rights has operated in new and old democracies alike as an ethical thorn in the flesh of power, a constant reminder of their theoretical commitment (reflected in the acceptance of this rights language in the first place) that liberty and security should be available to all.

Does all this make human rights, in E. P. Thompson's words again, an 'unqualified good'?[47] The judgment has to be more mixed. So far as the delivery of social and economic rights is concerned, a commitment to the language of human rights has frequently manifestly failed to deliver wholescale the rich reading of liberty and security that it seems to promise. Signing up to a rights instrument or embracing the language of human rights within one's national system does not abolish the difficult political decisions that have to be made to bring such attractive outcomes about. Even where these rights are embedded as constitutional entitlements within national legal systems, this has not resulted in uniform, effective judicial employment of those standards to advance liberty and security for non-elites; a fact that is strongly evidenced by national experiences such as those of South Africa and Brazil.[48] We need at this stage to recall the weakness shown by most constitutional arrangements when it has come to the kinds of decisions needed to achieve any sort of substantive equality in even democratic states. Just as elected branches of government have failed to employ constitutional or other legal equality requirements to transform the prevailing privilege-benefitting status quo, judges too have generally been reluctant to employ or apply a notion of equality that their political colleagues have either disregarded or resolutely avoided.

More surprisingly perhaps, the language of human rights, and in particular that of civil and political rights, has not done as much as might have been expected (given its seeming commitment to universality and non-discrimination) to protect radical political speech and revolutionary activity generally from the sort of state control that, as we have seen, is so easily justified under both the Hobbesian and the republican forms of government. *Salus populi suprema lex* operates here as well. Foreshadowed in US case law which as we have seen denied First Amendment protection to Communist and anti-war speech, neither German guarantees of constitutional rights nor commitments to freedom of association and expression in the European Convention on Human Rights could save the German Communist Party from being banned in the Federal Republic in the 1950s. Italian radicals found themselves similarly inhibited in their critique of the post-war order established in their country. The commitment made then to property rights and to due process made revolutionary action next to impossible, as the radical delegates vainly complained at the Italian convention where such matters were finally agreed.[49] Subsequent rights instruments find themselves similarly equipped to resist by force unacceptably subversive efforts at political activity. Post-colonial and post-Soviet states in particular may all have committed themselves to frameworks of rights which have seemed to prioritize political activism without asking first about the acceptability of what is being said, but all such documents also invariably contain exceptions for what is 'necessary in a democratic society' or for such 'reasonable limits' as are 'prescribed by law' or some such exculpatory formulae. Indeed with their guarantees of privacy, due process and above all of property, often overseen by judges who in these situations have seen no problems in their active involvement, the deployment of the language (and the law) of civil and political rights has often seemed as likely to support the protection of inequality as work towards its elimination.

The depressing truth has been that rights instruments have not necessarily guaranteed the rights of those on the outside for whom Hobbesian liberty has been a distant dream. Nor has all this rights talk protected those whose advocacy on behalf of the marginalized has been so robust as to involve radical critique of the systemic inequality inherent in the model of democratic government with which they are confronted (and in turn confront). To put it frankly: human rights law does not inevitably put food on the table or get homes to the homeless. Indeed, it may serve to allow dissent to be controlled in a way that can be presented as human-rights-legitimate. In this way, human rights exactly mirrors the residual approach to liberty that I have just been discussing. For the rich and the ordinarily affluent, human rights law is an ethical accessory to a good life rather than the deliverer of any kind of liberty that is not already enjoyed as a simple matter of course. It protects a freedom of speech which it never occurs to its proponents to exercise other than within predictable and conventional parameters. But step outside the preordained boundaries, and you risk being dealt with as harshly under human rights law as you would be were such laws not available to you. Protestors in shopping malls find they can be legitimately removed.[50] May Day protestors in London in 2000 can be held for hours ('kettled') in a way which the courts later insist was in full accordance with their right to liberty.[51]

## Universalism under Attack

Let me conclude this chapter by summarizing the main lines of the argument of this book. The democratic turn which began in England and then slowly rolled out across the world in the decades (even centuries) that followed was marked by a substantive commitment to the delivery of liberty and security for all. The republican ideal embraced ever-widening circles of stakeholders within its benign remit as the breadth of what it meant to be 'self-governed' expanded to bring ever more people within its community of electors. Driven by the principle of representative (democratic) government, this surge towards a liberty and security that was available to all was supported by the detached impartiality of the rule of law and the ethical ambition of the laws (and language) of human rights. None of these forces for universalism was able to escape the context from which each had emerged however. The baggage of a past of unfairness and inequality, of the partisan allocation of liberty and security in an inequitable world, clung on to each. Even at their height in any given society, the guarantees of democracy, law and human rights were always vulnerable to being undercut in the interests of the few.

It was exactly this flaw which made it possible for democracy, liberty, legality and human rights to fit so well within societies that had organized themselves along primarily capitalist lines. It was a two-way deal: universal liberty was respected as long as the invisible lines that inhibited any seriously radical challenge to the state were not crossed while on the other side – for those with power and money – it was important not to resist democratic efforts to deliver security for all, even though this would necessarily come at a price in terms of a small downward readjustment of wealth and a slight narrowing of opportunity (due to the increased social mobility that came from facilitating opportunity for all). The democratic era, then, was to this extent arguably the creature of a grand bargain between capitalism and its ideological opponents: we'll give you a little more than the usual crumbs and allow a few more of you than usual to clamber on to the table from time to time but we will continue to resist your using the liberty you have won to question the fundamentals of how the whole meal has been set up.

If the liberty and security that emerged from this was the result of a bargain rather than any ideological conviction, then it was always vulnerable to re-negotiation in light of events. Even as early as the 1970s in some parts of South America new versions of liberty were being experimented with, approaches to human freedom and security which were marked by a more or less explicit rejection of universalism in favour of the market. Around the same time, the United States began its slow march away from the egalitarianism that had been such a feature of the New Deal politics that had dominated two generations of policy-making, from President Roosevelt in the 1930s through to Richard Nixon and the oil crisis of the early 1970s. The shift towards the new model of a more market-based and less state-oriented approach to governance gathered momentum in the 1980s (with President Reagan and UK Prime Minister Margaret Thatcher being early cheerleaders) and then took off with the collapse of Soviet-sponsored socialism in 1989. With the 'neo-liberalism' that then increasingly took hold, both in the established as well as the new democracies, a different, more partial account of liberty and security began slowly to re-emerge from the pre-democratic shadows. Perhaps this was coincidence, perhaps causal. Certainly resistance to the egalitarian implications of democracy had always been present: that is the point behind much of this chapter. But it learnt to tame itself, to hang back, restricting itself to that resistance exercise of its veto only when radicalism threatened to get out of control. In recent years, however, selective accounts of liberty and security have become more brazen, the debt to the poor less likely to be acknowledged, the focus of liberty much more likely to be expressed in libertarian terms.

But just as the move to universalism could not shed its past, neither can the radically changed circumstances of the present moment easily dispense with the baggage upon which its model society has been built. The markets had triumphed but the home societies from which they had captured the world continue to bear unmistakeable traces of earlier concessions to socialism: the valuing of equality; the commitment to democracy; the move to universal human rights; in the language of this book the ostensible commitment to liberty and security for all. The widely accepted idea of the rule of law (across the political spectrum) has also meant that the legal shape these ideals had taken cannot be simply disregarded.

This is the space out of which has emerged neo-democracy. The answer has been to seem to have it both ways. Increasingly societies have organized themselves as places of great (and rising inequality) with nevertheless apparently strong commitments to democracy and human rights, supported by the impartial demands of a rule of law that claims to stand above politics as a guarantor of freedom. It is when no fair-minded observer not intent on fooling him- or herself can avoid the mismatch between the facts of inequality and the forms of freedom that we know we are living in a neo-democratic world: poverty on the rise; the emergence of super-rich classes; the elections always won by the same crowd; the court judgments that go only one way; the human rights ethic that is applauded in the abstract and ignored on the streets; the external inspectors that change next to nothing.

A potential presence in democracy from the outset, and arguably given impetus by the wholesale neo-liberal turn in the 1990s, this way of organizing the state has found itself being given a free rein in the first years of the third millennium. The attacks of 11 September 2001 put this narrow version of liberty and security back on the agenda of all states, and international and regional political organizations as well. It came at exactly the time when the powerful were increasingly inclined to redesign democracy to fit their increasingly brazen view of what liberty and security truly entailed. Resistance has been possible only through the best aspects of the residual universalist language of democracy, the rule of law and human rights – flawed though they were, here are to be found the best hopes we have for universal readings of liberty and security. It is to this battle of ideas, still ongoing, that I now turn, in the remaining chapters of this book.

# 3

# The Global Stage

## Security Predominant

On the day after the Al-Qaida assaults on New York, Washington and in Pennsylvania on 11 September 2001, the UN Security Council met to condemn 'in the strongest terms' these 'horrifying terrorist attacks' and to call on all states and the international community to 'work together urgently' – to 'redouble their efforts' it said – to 'prevent and suppress' such acts. As for itself, the Council expressed 'its readiness to take all necessary steps to respond to the terrorist attacks . . . and to combat all forms of terrorism, in accordance with its responsibilities under the Charter of the United Nations'.[1] What the last of these entailed became apparent just sixteen days later with the promulgation, on 28 September 2001, of Resolution 1373, still the key document so far as international engagement with security is concerned in the post-11 September world that we have since come to inhabit. Acting against 'threats to international peace and security' under Chapter VII of the UN Charter (and therefore availing of the element of compulsion inherent upon states under that part of the Charter), the Security Council required all countries to act in various ways against terrorism, including in regards to its financing and the support that might previously have been shown by some of them for 'terrorist' groups. An 'intensifying and accelerating' of efforts at international co-operation was likewise demanded,[2] together with action against suspected terrorist asylum seekers (albeit only 'in conformity with the relevant provisions of national and international law, including international standards of human rights').[3]

To make all this tick over in a more coherent way than usual, the Security Council made a further important decision, establishing a 'committee . . . consisting of all members of the Council, to monitor implementation of this resolution, with the assistance of appropriate expertise' and it went on to call for all member states to report to this body 'no later than 90 days from the date of adoption of this resolution and thereafter according to a timetable to be proposed by the Committee, on the steps they have taken to implement this resolution'.[4] Further resolutions reaffirming 1373 followed the atrocities committed in Bali on 12 October 2002, the hostage taking in Moscow that occurred the same month, the attacks in Kenya in November 2002, in Bogotá in February 2003, in Istanbul in November that same year, and in Madrid on 11 March 2004 (albeit wrongly attributing this attack to the Basque 'terrorist group ETA').[5]

Two weeks after the last of these attacks, the Security Council toughened up its position as the enforcer of 1373, accepting a report by its committee (now known as the Counter-Terrorism Committee or 'CTC') on that body's 'revitalization' and creating a 'Counter-Terrorism Committee Executive Directorate' (or 'CTED') as a 'special political mission' with an executive director and a new team of international civil servants to assist this officer.[6] After the London bombings of 7 July 2005 the usual condemnatory resolution[7] was followed within three weeks by yet a further and this time much more detailed intervention, adding to the range of Resolution 1373 obligations and including the expression of a new concern, about 'the use of various media, including the Internet, by Al-Qaida, Osama bin Laden, and the Taliban, and their associates, including for terrorist propaganda and inciting terrorist violence'.[8]

The UN stands at the apex of our commitment to broad understandings of liberty and security. In many ways it is the epitome of the drive to universalism that I earlier described as having gathered momentum after World War Two. It is true that even in the 1990s the organization had come under pressure from a fast-growing neo-liberal consensus, particularly on account of its insistence on the legal nature of human rights obligations (including economic and social rights) at a time when the policies of many states were increasingly delivering the very opposite of this (albeit – of course and as we have seen – in the name of a supposed greater freedom). There had through the 1980s and 1990s also been pressure for more action on terrorism as well, not least because of the importance of the idea in Israeli (and therefore US) political circles. But even having acknowledged this background, it is not always appreciated quite how large-scale the post-11 September shift in UN priorities was, or how the very idea of what we mean by the UN has, in this area at least, undergone a dramatic change.

So far as the change in the UN is concerned, the preamble to its founding Charter of 1945 had spoken of four goals in particular: 'to save succeeding generations from the scourge of war'; 'to reaffirm faith in fundamental human rights, in the dignity and worth of the human person, in the equal rights of men and women and of nations large and small'; 'to establish conditions under which justice and respect for the obligations arising from treaties and other sources of international law [could] be maintained', and 'to promote social progress and better standards of life in larger freedom'. This last phrase 'in larger freedom' captures neatly what this book is about, a rich kind of liberty for all, rooted in universal rather than partial security. But the UN initiatives I have described right at the start of this chapter have next to nothing to say about at least the last three of these foundational goals. As we have seen in resolution 1373, human rights did get a brief passing mention (in the context of clamping down on asylum-seeking 'terrorists'), but beyond that nothing. Even more dramatically, the Security Council has created a whole bureaucracy (the CTC and the CTED) to drive its counter-terrorism agenda deep into the heart of each and every one of the member states. Whereas in the past these national administrations could have expected a committee delegation or visiting rapporteur from the UN to concentrate on human rights and the delivery of a 'larger freedom', now there are also these new international civil servants, travelling about the world insisting that it is the counter-terrorism agenda that should be central.

It is not hard to guess which UN engagement national governments – even democratic but certainly authoritarian ones – prefer. This takes me to what we mean when we talk here of the counter-terrorism activities of the United Nations. It is not the General Assembly that we need to have in mind but rather the Security Council, that small group of states at the top of the UN system with its five permanent members (the US, Russia, China, France and the UK) and its passing representatives from other nations. This body has seized the right to insist on legislation on a global scale to counter the threat from terrorism – and in doing so it offers no comprehensive guidance on what 'terrorism' means (for instance in a Security Council resolution or other statement), albeit while insisting in the way I have just been describing on robust state action against such (uncertainly defined) actions.

Here is a vital hostage to fortune insofar as political freedom – a vital part of the liberty of the many – is concerned. Left uncontrolled, the remit of terrorism can quickly extend beyond its core element of indiscriminate criminal assaults on civilians to be made to cover all sorts of conduct that on a closer look is well removed from the central thrust of the damning label that is now being affixed to it. Take the approach of the International Convention for the Suppression of the Financing of Terrorism 1999[9] to which Res 1373 referred specifically when it called on member states to sign up to the UN's corpus of anti-terrorism treaties.[10] Here the conduct covered by all of the nine specific conventions on terrorism-related matters was designated 'terrorist' without any further discussion of motive behind any such actions (hijack; certain kinds of kidnapping; etc.)[11] – it was only where the relevant actions fell outside those conventions that the kind of injury ('an act intended to cause death or serious bodily injury to a civilian, or to any other person not taking an active part in the hostilities in a situation of armed conflict') and the purpose behind it ('to intimidate a population, or to compel a Government or an international organization to do or to abstain from doing any act') came into play.[12] And that Convention is a model of discipline compared to the fortunately failed effort of the General Assembly to produce a comprehensive definition of 'terrorism', something on which an ad hoc committee has been working since 1996, albeit consistently managing to avoid coming to any conclusion despite the impetus of the various terrorist catastrophes that would surely have served as an incentive to action in any other body less committed to inertia than the inner sanctums of the General Assembly of the UN.

Why do I say 'fortunately failed'? The breaking point for many states has been the implicit rejection of all subversive political violence – something which they see as part and parcel of what they are being asked to agree and to which for reasons of their own particular histories and their support for specific liberation movements in various territories (e.g. Palestine) they feel unable to sign up. But a further real danger in the draft Convention lies in what does seem to have been agreed – a definition of terrorism of dangerous width, covering not just what we saw embraced within the 1999 Convention but going on to include both 'serious damage to public or private property, including a place of public use, a State or government facility, a public transportation system, an infrastructure facility or to the environment' and also (as an alternative) damage to any of these places, facilities or environment which results in 'or is likely to result in major economic loss', just so long as (in each case) 'the purpose of the conduct, by its nature or context, is to intimidate a population, or to compel a Government or an international organization to do or abstain from doing any act.'[13] There are various ancillary offences as well and a general requirement for states to establish criminal offences along the lines of the definition. No distinction is made between democratic and authoritarian or totalitarian states – Sweden is on a par with North Korea or Burma so far as the draft Convention is concerned. True, draft Article 4 exempts actions occurring exclusively within individual states but this is a mere nod in the direction of the UN's requirement to have a transnational dimension to its operations – it is hard to see states legislating for terrorism crimes while exempting those of their subjects they deem most dangerous solely because they operate exclusively against them.

For all its faults, at least the draft Convention has been the subject of discussion across the various nations that make up the UN: no doubt this collective dimension explains why it seems to have got irretrievably stuck in a definitional mire from which there would appear to be no prospect of escape. After the attacks of 11 September 2001, and under immense pressure from an already hostile United States, the Security Council clearly felt that it had no alternative other than to seize the initiative for itself. Even with a clear and limited definition this would have been problematic from the point of view of the three elements to universal freedom that, as we have seen, form the basis of the argument in this book for liberty and security for all: there is no democratic dimension to the decision-making (other than – almost trivially – the extent to which a few of the Security Council members have varying kinds of democratic mandates); neither is there any judicial oversight of the consequences that flow from Security Council action in this field (which has been an important factor in some positive developments on this to which we turn shortly); and the protection of human rights is largely ignored.

In the next chapter we turn to each of these points so far as they have played out in individual states – as the then UN Special Rapporteur on the Promotion and Protection of Human Rights and Fundamental Freedoms Martin Scheinin put it in a report in December 2005,[14] '[c]alls by the international community to combat terrorism, without defining the term . . . carries the potential for unintended human rights abuses and even the deliberate misuse of the term'.[15] As we shall see, this story is a depressing one of blatantly authoritarian and neo-democratic governments being handed a UN tool to position themselves in a way that (in the words of Scheinin again) 'results in the unintentional international legitimization of conduct undertaken by oppressive regimes'.[16] This important story of how universal liberty and security have been distorted worldwide by the opportunity opened up by the UN counter-terrorism drive is, as I say, for later. First however we need to look at ways in which the UN Security Council itself has directly intervened in the domestic legal frameworks of its member States so as to attack the liberty of the few in the name of the security of the many. It is not an edifying story albeit it remains an unfinished one, with the sad possibility lurking however that ongoing reforms have made things worse not better.

## Blacklists

The UN has long used sanctions as part of its medley of responses to state wrongdoing. An early example was in the 1960s, against what was to become Zimbabwe with first a non-binding resolution in 1965[17] calling on states 'to do their utmost in order to break all economic relations with Southern Rhodesia, including an embargo on oil and petroleum products' and then a later resolution invoking Chapter VII[18] and setting up a committee tasked with monitoring the implementation of the sanctions regime thereby established. With the Cold War over the Security Council found itself able to make use of this sanction weapon almost with abandon through the 1990s, against – for example – Iraq (for its invasion and occupation of Kuwait)[19] and various governmental and non-governmental entities in Afghanistan, Haiti, Liberia, Rwanda, Sudan and the former Yugoslavia. Trade in certain commodities was banned ('blood diamonds') and sometimes countries found their diplomatic presence being forcibly scaled back (as happened with Sudan). The idea of going after key personnel was present quite early on, with bans on air links and/or the travel of elites being imposed on Iraq, the former Yugoslavia, Libya, Haiti, Angola, Sudan, Sierra Leone and Afghanistan, and the financial assets of governments or particular individuals being targeted in Iraq, the former Yugoslavia, Libya, Haiti, Angola and Afghanistan.

As the 1990s proceeded, and particularly on account of the effect of sanctions on the innocent in Iraq and Haiti, the attraction of targeted moves against particular personnel ('smart sanctions') grew in the eyes of policy-makers: much better to be getting the particular bad-guys than simply making things worse for the unfortunate peoples over whom they ruled. The Security Council took six years – from 1998 through to 2003 – over a series of engagements (the Interlaken, Bonn-Berlin and Stockholm processes) which were designed to develop an effective means of implementing targeted sanctions.[20] But of course the closer these interventions got to particular people, the more they threatened to impact negatively on their liberty in a way that mimicked criminal or civil proceedings – but without any of the equivalent protections to be found in either such regimes.

The key escalation came with Resolution 1267, promulgated on 15 October 1999 against the Taliban regime in Afghanistan for its harbouring of 'international terrorists and their organizations' in general and its continuing refusal to turn over Osama bin Laden to the proper authorities for trial in particular. Acting under Chapter VII, flight bans and financial freezing orders were imposed, and a committee ('the 1267 committee') set up to oversee the whole operation. With a bureaucracy now to support it, targeted sanctions quickly took off – on 19 December 2000 Osama bin Laden himself was included with the 1267 committee being asked to maintain 'an updated list, based on information provided by States and regional organizations, of the individuals and entities designated as being associated with Osama bin Laden, including those in the Al-Qaida organization'.[21] A monitoring group and 'Sanctions Enforcement Support

Team' were established in July 2001[22] and after the attacks on 11 September 2001, there were – inevitably – a slew of further initiatives, broadening the range of those potentially within these sanctions' regimes and deepening the level of UN oversight of their proper enforcement.[23] By July 2005 the latest of these resolutions was referring to the 'consolidated list' of blacklisted individuals and organizations while setting out new and tougher ways in which to force countries to take punitive action against those on it.[24]

But how did you get on these lists? And – just as important – how could you get off? In the early days it was simply a matter of states pitching certain names and/or organizations for inclusion, without any serious oversight or evaluation of the evidential basis for the decision. Naturally no person of any influence or importance in the process thought for one moment that any person like themselves – much less somebody they knew – would be likely to find themselves pitched into this legal black hole; taking their own liberty for granted, their consuming interest was with their own (and their own kind's) security. And naturally some states at least yielded to the temptation to construe – how best to put this? – somewhat loosely the degree of connection with 'international terrorists' (a term we should remind ourselves that is nowhere defined) that was required to bring a person within reach of sanctions. The effect soon became apparent, and was well detailed in, among other places, an excellent report in 2007 by Dick Marty for the Committee on Legal Affairs and Human Rights of the Parliamentary Assembly of the Council of Europe.[25]

To take just a few examples, Youssef Nada was a 77-year-old man living in a tiny Italian commune in Switzerland who found himself both prevented from leaving his home area and also unable to access his financial accounts – despite being a senior figure in the world of banking. The problem for Mr Nada probably lay in the sort of bank that he ran; the Al Taqwa Islamic Investment Bank was associated with the Moslem Brotherhood as was Mr Nada himself and in both of these capacities he had found himself at odds with the then authoritarian leader of his country of original nationality, Hosni Mubarak of Egypt. Now, the important point for our purposes here is that Nada has found it entirely impossible to challenge this sudden but covert destruction of his liberty. Swiss proceedings of the conventional criminal sort had been dropped for lack of evidence, and similar efforts to deploy the ordinary law against him in Italy also failed when even the prosecutor assigned to the case decided there was not enough evidence to sustain his investigation. But the blacklisting, entirely unaffected by the need for any kind of public demonstration of an evidential foundation, carried on regardless. The Swiss courts were sympathetic but felt they could do nothing as the authorities had been acting under the direct mandate of the UN. The Swiss parliament then became exercised on his behalf and further proceedings were launched, this time before the European Court of Human Rights, with that body sending a number of questions about the matter to the Swiss authorities on 12 March 2009. Then as suddenly as he had appeared on the list Nada was taken off – on 23 September 2009, almost eight years after he had been put on. All his associated companies were likewise delisted in the course of the following six months. It was left to the US Treasury to explain in rather Delphic terms in relation to the case that the US supports 'the removal of those individuals who are no longer appropriate for listing pursuant to that specific regime'.[26] Of course as is so often the case it had been the US who had put Nada on the list just as it was they who decided to take him off – as we have already noted, the UN role in the 1267 process is more often than not as a mere cipher for the unaccountable wishes of its member states.

It can only be imagined what kind of fuss would have been made had powers like these been exercised against a mainstream banking figure in the western world, a CEO of Goldman Sachs, for example, or of Morgan Stanley. Recalling a point made in the last chapter in a different context, the furore would perhaps have been at least as noisy as that generated by successful white businessmen in Britain whenever they find themselves facing extradition to the US for alleged crimes, shock at the draconian nature of the law mixed with horror that it is being applied to this sort of person being the main drivers (assisted by money of course) of public indignation. But whatever about his saying he was Italian, Nada was just another Arab, or Moslem or whatever it was – and he was involved in something called an Islamic Bank. His liberty is therefore not ours; our security must trump his freedom every time; these blacklists only apply to people like him so affect not one jot how 'we' experience freedom.

The People's Mojahadeen Organization of Iran (PMOI) is a similar case, albeit this time involving a political association rather than an individual. The PMOI was established in order to replace the Shah with a democratic system of government, and so it was hardly surprising that it found the theocracy established under the Ayatollah Khomeini that followed the downfall of the Shah not at all to its taste. It went on to co-found the National Council of Resistance of Iran thereby annoying not the US this time (unsurprisingly) but rather the British – with the result that the organization was placed on a blacklist established by the EU as part of its collective response to the requirements of UNSC 1373 (rather than, on this occasion, 1267 – blacklists had by now taken on a life of their own outside their original context). The EU courts managed to get hold of the case and once confronted with how the thing had been done the EU's Court of First Instance (CFI) was quick to condemn the procedural vacuum in which it found the listing had been made – there had to be some reasons given and at least a rudimentary notification that such an event is about to happen or has just occurred, and there must also be some kind of opportunity for judicial review. The Court annulled the decision, only for the EU Council to relist the PMOI with a minimum set of reasons (supplied by the UK government). The organization was then drawn into a long game of legal ping-pong, winning in the UK against a national listing, succeeding in its challenge to the EU relisting process, fighting off a late effort by France to list them afresh, and being eventually and finally delisted on 26 January 2009.[27] It has been easy to forget along the way that these describe themselves (and are supported by many) as the *democratic* opposition to the pseudo-democracy of theocratic Iran.

The Nada and PMOI cases are only two among many. Where would either have got to without the threat or (in PMOI's case) actual intervention of the courts? The invaluable feature of judicial engagement in cases such as these is that the judges are directed by law not instinct, and these days one of the happier of our democratic legacies is that the law appears to guarantee the same procedural safeguards to all. Selective liberty is no longer explicit as it was in – say – John Locke's day: in these ostensibly egalitarian times, we are all supposed to be able to enjoy it, whatever our original nationality and whatever the cause we choose to pursue. This takes us to the heart of the matter so far as the rule of law is concerned, why for all its faults (many discussed in the last chapter) it is an invaluable ally of universal liberty. Whatever their political persuasion or laypersons' views on security, lawyers and judges tend to regard the equality of the legal process and the universality of the human rights that this process is designed to secure, as not (merely) for show but as substantial, as promises to be delivered upon rather than ruses to assuage our consciences. These are legacies of our earlier unambiguous commitment to universal liberty. It is exactly because the courts take procedure and human rights at face value, as available to all, that those involved in individual decisions on security grounds try desperately to stay clear of them. The world in which they move is one in which judgments about risk prevail, impacts on individual suspects are not central to any such assessment, and procedural requirements are impediments to effective decision-making, not safeguards against error.

## Fight-Back

The role of the European courts in challenging the blacklisting regime has been heroic. Their finest moment came not in *PMOI* but in another case, one involving Yassin Abdullah

Kadi. Kadi and the Al Barakaat International Foundation of Sweden (part of the 'Hawala' banking system used by the Somalian diaspora to transfer funds internationally) had been put on a US Treasury Department blacklist as early as 12 October 2001, as 'specially designated global terrorists', with a particularly lurid web site describing Kadi as 'one of the dirty dozen of leading terror financiers being investigated by the CIA.'[28] Seven days later, both Kadi and Al Barakaat were placed on the 1267 list as associates of Osama bin Laden, and the EU – choosing as with the PMOI to discharge the UN obligations of Member States on their behalf – promptly brought him within their own fast-developing sanctions regime (via its EC regulatory powers). The usual throttling economic controls followed. As with Nada, it is difficult to imagine that there was much official thought given to Kadi and Al Barakaat as the names moved swiftly from list to list. While there was no international mechanism with which to challenge the UN decision, however, the EU engagement gave both the man and the bank a chance similar to that availed of by the PMOI, and on 18 December 2001 they launched a legal challenge seeking to annul the relevant EU regulation on the basis that it infringed their fundamental rights, specifically the right to be heard, the right to respect for their property and the right to effective judicial review.

The omens for the case were initially not good. It was quite something to ask a regional court to nullify the impact of a UN Chapter VII-backed requirement within its legal space. The European Court of Human Rights – which you might have thought would have been happy to take a lead on a case like this – had already bottled the challenge, in a decision made just before the *Kadi* and *Al Barakaat* matters came before the CFI.[29] So the CFI surprised few when on 28 September 2005 it ruled against both applicants.[30] The Court simply felt that it did not have jurisdiction to challenge the UN in this way, which despite all the arguments against presented by lawyers for the two men, was exactly what they thought they were being asked to do. True, if the UN Security Council resolution was truly heinous, reflecting an attack on the fundamentals of the international legal order (or *ius cogens*) then things might be different – but that was far from being the case here. The two applicants promptly appealed to the main EU court, the European Court of Justice (ECJ) and as part of that body's usual procedures a report was commissioned by a legal expert to assist it in its deliberations, an officer called an Advocate-General. There are eight such functionaries, all required to act publicly and impartially. This is perhaps the very pinnacle of achievement for a European lawyer, arguably even more prestigious (and maybe also more influential) than being one of the 27 judges on the court itself. Among the eight was Miguel Poiares Maduro, a Portugese scholar coming to the end of his term of office.

On 18 January 2008 he presented his opinion to the court. It was one of those remarkable moments when an important figure challenges in simple and clear language an orthodoxy that had appeared unimpeachable until the very moment of its being toppled. To Maduro the issue was very simple: it is for the ECJ (and the CFI) to 'determine the effect of international obligations within the Community legal order by reference to conditions set by Community law'. Of course the EU could not and should not suspend its framework of rights protection on the mere say-so of an international body, however august that organization might be. And clearly here the UN had not even begun to address the issues of fairness and of due process that were before the court. Things might have been different 'had there been a genuine and effective mechanism of judicial control by an independent tribunal at the level of the United Nations' since this would have 'released the Community from an obligation to provide for judicial control of implementing measures that apply within the Community legal order.' But there being no such system of accountability the ECJ should now, Maduro thought, step into the breach. And on 3 September 2008, the Court made a remarkable ruling, following Advocate-General Maduro on all the key issues.

The CFI had been wrong to genuflect to the UN and the Advocate-General had been right to insist on the protection of fundamental rights. On the facts before it, the Court was clear that 'the rights of the defence, in particular the right to be heard, and the right to effective judicial review of those rights, were patently not respected' and the complete failure of the EC regulation to include any procedure for 'communicating the evidence justifying the inclusion of the names of the persons' affected by the listing was another fatal flaw. As with the PMOI litigation this was just the start of things for Mr Kadi. While Al Barakaat was eventually delisted, Kadi has been back and forth to court since, arguing (successfully) that his continued delisting is invalid notwithstanding having (now) been given a kind of summary set of reasons, and also finding himself advised to launch a case in the US against the authorities there, the originators of all his troubles. Into the gap created by the *Kadi* case a whole range of similarly aggrieved listees have now poured. The European Court of Human Rights has also involved itself, ruling in favour of Youssef Nada in a recent case.[31] The listing procedure has become highly problematic so far as the legal space occupied by the European Union has been concerned. True, the UN intervention has not been the subject of direct challenge with it being the various translations of the blacklists into EC law which has given the ECJ and CFI judges the opportunity to act. But it is certainly rather formalistic of the ECJ in *Kadi* (and subsequently) to claim rather blandly that the case involves no challenge to external authority.

## Drifting beyond Law

So how has the UN reacted to this challenge to its global writ? Here we come to an important point in the development of the law from the point of view of the argument in this book. The right thing to do from the perspective of democracy, human rights and the rule of law – true liberty for all – would be to abolish the whole system. Its failures are evident for all to see: the absence of any specific criminal charges; the reliance on confidential evidence; the lack of accountability and of even a modicum of due process in the decision to list; the large-scale negative impact of such decisions on the human rights of those made subject to them; and (it might be thought above all) the inability to challenge any such listing before a tribunal with even a passing resemblance to an independent court of law.

It is not as if the UN does not possess an alternative set of structures to deal with persons suspected of involvement in heinous terrorist activity. The UN Office on Drugs and Crime has issued a *Handbook on Criminal Justice Responses to Terrorism*[32] which is a model of the right kind of emphasis to take. Drafted with the assistance of policing and criminal justice experts, its opening sentence reveals immediately its perspective: 'An effective and prevention-focused response to terrorism should include a strong criminal justice element: one that is guided by a normative legal framework and embedded in the core principles of the rule of law, due process and respect for human rights.'[33] Of course a 'comprehensive criminal justice response'[34] will involve close international and regional co-operation, just as it may necessitate the development of new criminal offences and wider police powers at state level. But the emphasis on the 'criminal' is a perpetual reminder of the need not to assume guilt, to approach even these sorts of police enquiries with an open mind, and to build cases that are intended to satisfy independent-minded judges (and, depending on the system, sometimes juries) rather than partisan ministers (or their security and even media advisers) shouting for action from the sidelines. The criminal model is robust in its determination to provide security for all, but in a way that respects the liberty not only of the powerful but of all that come to its attention, whether they be citizens or visitors, part of a well-settled community or members of a vulnerable minority or (even, and particularly) suspects of serious wrongdoing.

The Security Council has not chosen the option of abolition. Instead and in reaction to the cases we have been discussing, as well as the very strongly critical views voiced by many in academe and in the legal professions, it has chosen the path of reform. Ever more intricate processes have been constructed so as to give a greater sense of fairness – sufficient it is hoped to cause the courts and civil society to back off, or at least moderate their criticisms – but without delivering anything remotely close to the procedural guarantees that you would naturally expect if your property were being taken, your freedom of movement curtailed, your business closed down by operation of the ordinary law. This, then, in the language we are using in this book, is a move to neo-democracy that we can track as it happens, a shift to a system of quasi-criminal law with some of the appearances of freedom but precious little of its substance. Sadly it is emerging from within the very citadel of universal liberty and security, the UN itself.

As early as the Summer of 2005, in UNSC Resolution 1617,[35] member states were being asked to provide 'a statement of case describing the basis of the proposal' to list[36] and were also being requested 'to inform, to the extent possible, and in writing where possible, individuals and entities included in the Consolidated List of the measures imposed on them'.[37] Seventeen months later, UNSC Resolution 1730[38] established a 'Focal Point' within the Security Council secretariat to which affected individuals or entities could make delisting requests. The idea was that this Focal Point would then tell such aggrieved persons or organizations what they should do to push ahead with their petition, and would pass on their supplications to the relevant states. In due course it also fell to the Focal Point to inform them of the outcome of their request. A second resolution three days after Resolution 1730[39] tried to make the listing process a bit more open while also developing some criteria aimed at assisting in delisting – but so far as the second of these is concerned some of the things that the resolution mentioned ('mistake of identity'; 'the individual is deceased') served only to remind everyone of how riven with uncertainty the whole process was, while others ('the individual or entity no longer meets the criteria'; 'it has been affirmatively shown that the individual or entity has severed all association' with the proscribed groups) were too vague to be of any real value.

Six months after Maduro's intervention but before the ECJ ruling in *Kadi*, UNSC Resolution 1822[40] called for a much more open approach to listing on the part of member states, with use to be made of the 1267 committee's web site,[41] and the resolution went on (acknowledging implicitly how many mistakes had been made in the early days) to direct the committee to review all the names on the list within two years and annually thereafter.[42] It might have been *Kadi* that then stimulated the largest change in the procedure, in UNSC Resolution 1904,[43] doing away altogether with the Focal Point so far as the 1267 committee was concerned and creating a new Office of the Ombudsperson (to be occupied by 'an eminent individual of high moral character, impartiality and integrity with high qualifications and experience')[44] to assist that committee in its delisting work. All that the Ombudsperson does, however, is act as a kind of confidential advocate for the listed person or entity – the officer does not make the decision and nor is he or she allowed to divulge full details to the person or entity on behalf of whom he or she is acting.

Now of course the current incumbent, the Canadian judge Kimberley Prost, probably believes she is doing a good job, and there is no reason to doubt that within the constraints of the post she might well be.[45] It is perfectly possible that still further modifications and improvements will occur, such as those that took place in the Summer of 2011 with two further resolutions from the Security Council separating out the way in which Taliban and Al-Qaida suspected individuals and associates are treated and making it a bit easier for the Ombudsperson to achieve delisting in Al-Qaida cases.[46] But it is hard not to share the opinion of the outgoing UN Special Rapporteur on Human Rights and Terrorism Martin Scheinin that the changes do not 'remedy the human rights shortcomings [he had earlier] expressed in relation to the Consolidated List' Scheinin went on to explain why:

Due to the unsatisfactory level of due process guarantees such as disclosure of information and a right to an effective remedy, the strengthened role of the Ombudsperson is unlikely to satisfy national or European courts that the safeguards at the United Nations level are sufficient, so that these

courts could allow deference instead of exercising their jurisdiction over the national or European measures for the
implementation of the sanctions.[47]

At the end of his critique of the measures, even the
indefatigable Professor Scheinin is drawn into the making of
some suggestions as to how things could be put right, a bit
more due process here, some more powers for the Ombudsperson there. This is understandable. The blacklists seem to
be here to stay. The temptation on the part of the Prosts and
Scheinins of this world – courageous lawyers engaged in difficult and complex work in the public interest – is to make
the best of things, to work with rather than against the grain
of international opinion, seeking amelioration rather than
revolution. This is exactly how we move into the neo-democratic phase. Its manifestation in the international arena are
these blacklisting regimes, originally utterly outside all pre-
existing systems of law and respect for human rights, but
now being drawn slowly into them. This is in many ways a
good thing – the taming of earlier international banditry in
the interests of due process and individual rights, in other
words (as we consistently put it here) respect for the liberty
of all. But it is exactly these improvements that make the
system more entrenched, more difficult to dislodge. With the
Prosts and the Scheinins onside, those who continue to argue
for outright rejection are pushed increasingly to the margins.

Such critics stop being viewed as mainstream and reasonably sensible and become extremist people with an idée
fixe about blacklists: agitators who are never willing to compromise; people who just don't know when to call it a day.
Is a draw not good enough for them? Why endlessly pursue
total victory? This is how paradigm shifts come about. Consider the exact nature of the supposed success that critical
engagement has achieved here: a quasi-judicial process – one
with part of the form but little of the substance of criminal
proceedings – is all that lies between any of us and a life
thrown into turmoil by a barely accountable decision of
mainly anonymous figures from the shadowy world of
national security. But even putting it like that reminds us

of the central point of this chapter, indeed of this book as a whole: of course it won't happen to us, we think – we are not like Kadi, or Nada, or PMOI or any of the others. This universality is for show, the real purpose is what matters – and that is security for us even if it means little liberty for them. And, to protect us from having to acknowledge this, let us construct a system of pseudo due process and ersatz respect for human rights, so that we can pretend to care for all while not in fact doing so – global neo-democracy in action.

# 4

# The Enemy Within

## Alibi for Oppression

How should the UN Security Council's Counter-Terrorism Committee (CTC) go about its business of investigating the effectiveness of state responses to terrorism in the aftermath of the 11 September attacks? In the last chapter we saw how, starting with UNSC Resolution 1373, a range of dictates had come from that Council – all under Title VII and all therefore requiring to be followed – telling states what to do and how to do it, and within what kind of time frame. Indeed this is exactly why the CTC and its various administrative support teams were created – to add bite to the UN's enforcement capabilities. We said we would come back to the way this has been worked through across the world and now is the time to do so. The potential for abuse is obvious: there is no agreed international definition of terrorism; the breadth of UN requirements leaves plenty of scope for state abuse; and the absence (at least initially) of any acknowledgement of the dictates of international human rights law weakens this code's moral reach while at the same time equipping those opposed to its application with a new rationale for their defiance. All of this plays into the neo-democratic reconfiguration of liberty and security in ways that will now be discussed.

An early report by the then UN's Special Rapporteur on the Promotion and Protection of Human Rights and Fundamental Freedoms Martin Scheinin, which I have already referred to in passing in the last chapter, gives a sense of the extent of the problems that Resolution 1373 has caused.[1] While there were cases in which the CTC worked hard to make sure that the laws they were assisting states with drafting fitted within the human rights framework of the country in question, in other situations the CTC's proposals were resisted, precisely on the ground of the countervailing requirements of the state's human rights guarantees. In these latter cases, the CTC responded by engaging 'in a positive dialogue for the purpose of putting into operation counter-terrorism measures that at the same time comply with human rights'.[2] But there was also a final category of case discovered by the Special Rapporteur, where the CTC had been 'insensitive to human rights'[3] and – adding hugely to the worry – the state under scrutiny had been entirely happy about this, more than willing to collude in this marginalization of human rights at the insistence of the august UN. Thus was Belarus able to rely on CTC comments to argue for the legitimacy of practices in the field of criminal law enforcement that had earlier drawn stinging criticism from the human rights arm of the UN (and the NGO sector that polices the field as well).[4]

Now Belarus might be thought to be a special case – Europe's last 'outpost of tyranny' as the US were calling it at the time, and it is certainly true that the opportunities for legitimizing repression afforded by CTC pressure will be more openly received the less a country is under any of the normal human-rights-oriented pressure that is part and parcel of contemporary democracy.[5] This is indelibly tied up with the broader question of the extent to which anti-terrorism laws can be used in such places as the weapon of choice so far as the controlling of domestic dissent is concerned. Thus to stay with Belarus for a moment, in March 2012 the authorities felt able to defy an intervention by the UN's Human Rights Committee to execute two men for an explosion on the Minsk metro after a trial in which confessions were allegedly obtained after ill-treatment and various basics of procedural fairness were ignored.[6] Further east, the authorities in Tajikistan routinely deploy the same cover for the naked exercise of coercive power, as in the case in Spring 2012 in which a large number of alleged Islamic extremists were sentenced to long prison sentences for various terrorism-related offences after a closed trial.[7] The same type of state action followed shortly afterwards in Kazakhstan, this time with 47 convicted after secret trials.[8]

Here are three states detached from the constraints of a democratic polity and therefore delighted to be able to seize on an anti-terrorism bandwagon that the democratic states have themselves started rolling (with the great assistance of the UN, as the last chapter made clear). This is the context in which we should also take note of China. Its definition of terrorism (adopted as recently as 29 October 2011, in a decision passed by Standing Committee of the National People's Congress) is as follows:

> Activities that severely *endanger society* that have the goal of creating terror in society, endangering public security, or threatening state organs and international organizations and which, by the use of violence, sabotage, intimidation, and *other methods*, cause or are intended to cause human casualties, great loss to property, damage to public infrastructure, and *chaos in the social order*, as well as activities that incite, finance, or assist the implementation of the above activities *through any other means*.[9]

Interestingly the web site that provides the English version of this extraordinary, near-hysterical definition,[10] the Global Legal Monitor of the Law Library of Congress, also explains why the decision to set out a meaning for the term was made: '[t]here was previously no clear and precise definition of terrorist organizations, or of terrorist activities or terrorists, provided in domestic law, and the lack of clear definitions has hampered international cooperation in anti-terrorism efforts'. This decision 'has been passed to fill this gap'. No mention here of the ritual criticisms to which China is so often subjected in the US when it acts in a way that can be characterized as violating human rights, or to what it means when a one-party-state passes something. The distinction between local and international affairs which as we have seen Resolution 1373 sought to maintain has disappeared and China has procured for itself a handy new vehicle for domestic oppression. As the Global Legal Monitor remarks, citing article 4, '[t]he Decision also provides the procedure for making lists of terrorist organizations and terrorists: the leading state anti-terrorism agency will decide on and adjust the lists, and the lists will be published by the State Council public security department (ie the Ministry of Public Security)'.

It might even be possible that this legislative initiative flowed from a November 2009 agreement between China and the US to 'deepen counter-terrorism consultation and cooperation on an equal and mutually beneficial basis and to strengthen law-enforcement cooperation' – this had been the very first item in the US-China joint statement that followed 'in-depth, productive and candid' talks between the then still fairly new US president Barack Obama and his Chinese counterpart that occurred at that time in Beijing. Meanwhile, a few paragraphs further down in the joint statement we learn that '[b]oth sides recognized that the United States and China have differences on the issue of human rights.'[11]

As this last bland statement illustrates, countries like China (and certainly Belarus, Tajikistan and Kazakhstan as well) stand outside that triangle of commitments – to human rights; the rule of law; and democracy – that mark out the tendency towards universal liberty and security for which this book is arguing. Despite nods in the direction of such values (China's constitutional commitment to human rights for example,[12] or Belarus's constitutional guarantees of human rights),[13] there is in such places no worked-through trade-off between liberty and security: these are countries where a tiny elite prosper while the vast majority of the people look on in growing disgust. If these states have constitutional guarantees of democratic rights (Belarus's 'The state for the People!' appears above the constitution on the president's web site)[14] then it is as an obvious sham: such states either do not pretend to be democracies or are transparently pseudo-democracies rather than anything approaching the real thing. Sad though they are this book has little to say about them – all we can do is hope that circumstances make possible a change and that the opportunity is then seized.[15] But until that happens, the terrorism discourse is one that they can be relied upon gleefully to seize upon as a distraction from external criticism and a handy weapon against internal dissent.

## Dressing the Window

Leaving to one side now these pseudo-democracies, what of the large parts of the world that do indeed appear to be embracing (or at least making efforts to embrace) more genuine forms of democracy? As I said in Chapter 1, there has in the past twenty years or so been a strong movement in the direction of democracy across the whole globe, and this has affected not just the former colonies of the western powers but has cut through entire swathes of the once Communist world as well. These are places which now – and rather suddenly it would seem – are both seeking, and expected to commit themselves to, democracy in practice as well as in theory; in other words – and using again the language of this book – to search for liberty and security for all. It is clearly a big ask to expect of such states that they should dive from tyranny and/or colonial oppression straight into the deep end of true democratic deliberation, debate and open and fair elections with no intermediate difficulties along the way.

There is an important point to make here about the difference between democratic structure and democratic culture: the first needs the second to make its design work since without such cultural support democratic constitutions can quickly decline into frameworks for tyranny, albeit ones in which the old authoritarianism finds itself now hidden behind a facade of freedom. Closing the gap between culture and structure would have been difficult in many of these newly emerging democratic polities even if conditions had proved to be entirely harmonious, and world support always unqualifiedly forthcoming – the governing precedents set by former rulers were invariably bad; local communities had often been divided as a way of exerting control; and (with the exception of eastern and central European states which have benefitted from contiguity to the EU) few efforts were ever made to lift newly liberated nations out of the mires of poverty and injustice in which their former masters had invariably left them. The primacy of capitalism since 1989 has caused further tensions, with the unequal accumulations of wealth celebrated by this mode of economic activity sitting oddly with the proclaimed egalitarianism of the form of government – representative democracy – supposedly best suited to it.

So it is hardly surprising that the transition to true democracy, to liberty and security for all, did not prove to be easy, even in the 1990s. Then along came 11 September 2001, the UN's reaction to it and the response of the established former colonial powers in the West (on which more in the next chapter). In exploring how the post-colonial and post-totalitarian states – already insecure in their move towards true democratic culture; already under pressure from their embracing of a capitalist system inimical to fairness for all – have reacted to the opportunity afforded to them both by the terrorism threat in general and by the new UN pressure to develop and expand their counter-terrorism laws in particular, we are able to see happening right in front of our eyes the shift to neo-democracy that we discussed in Chapter 2 and considered in relation to the UN in Chapter 3. By this – recalling earlier discussions – I mean the construction of a system in which liberty is enjoyed by the few and security in its fullest sense is available only to the elite, but (and here it is different from pseudo-democracies like Belarus) this is now occurring in a plausible framework that all the while appears to guarantee not only democracy and the rule of law but protection for fundamental freedom as well, and which (as part of this claim to credibility) frequently submits itself to external supervision. There are uncertainties at the edges, of course, and the trends we see in these states may well have emerged even without the UN impetus delivered after the 11 September attacks. But there can be little doubt of the role of the fear of terrorism as a facilitator of this worrying transition to neo-democracy.

Consider the example of Russia. Here is a country of some 138 million people with an elected president and a state Duma (or Parliament) which is also elected. The constitution describes (in article 1) Russia as a 'democratic federal law-bound State with a Republican form of government'.[16] Article 2 proclaims that 'Man, his rights and freedoms are the supreme value. The recognition, observance and protection of the rights and freedoms of man and citizen shall be the obligation of the State. 'No fewer than 48 articles are then devoted (in the second chapter of the Constitution) to the 'rights and freedoms of man and citizen'. The series of guarantees there set out paint a picture of a Nirvana in which liberty and security are available to all in their richest conceivable form: not only criminal law safeguards and civil and political rights but social and economic guarantees as well (health; education; home; social security; etc.) and even a fairly ambitious range of environmental guarantees ('the right to a favourable environment' in article 42 and an obligation 'to preserve nature and the environment' in article 58). Just in case the reader has any doubts and thinks perhaps that this is a UDHR-type unenforceable fantasy, article 46 declares that 'Everyone shall be guaranteed judicial protection of his rights and freedoms', with article 120 affirming that '[j]udges shall be independent and submit only to the Constitution and the federal law'. It is not surprising that given this kind of quality constitution, there were few difficulties about Russia becoming the 39th member state of the Council of Europe in 1996, and ratifying the European Convention on Human Rights, as the country did on 5 May

1998. So from that date individuals within the state could take their government to the European Court of Human Rights in Strasbourg if they could show themselves to be credible victims of Convention-based human rights abuses, so long as they had exhausted the plethora of local remedies promised them by Russia's state-of-the-art constitutional guarantees.

So much for what is on paper. The reality appears however to be rather different. Even the normally cautious British Foreign Office points to doubts about elections, reporting the description by the Organization for Security and Co-operation in Europe (OSCE) and the Council of Europe of Duma elections in 2007 as 'neither free nor fair', with both unbalanced media coverage and an unfair use of state resources strongly favouring the governing party.[17] Furthermore:

> While human rights and civil freedoms have improved significantly since the collapse of the USSR, concerns remain about respect for basic rights in Russia. Despite some minor reforms and encouraging public statements there has been no evidence of systemic, far-reaching change. Continuing negative trends include restrictions on freedom of assembly and expression, harassment and obstruction of NGOs and journalists and racial discrimination and violence. Frequent reports of grave human rights abuses in the North Caucasus continue.[18]

It is in this latter region and particularly in Chechnya (where '[t]here are continuing, credible allegations of extra-judicial killings, forced disappearances, torture, rape and arbitrary detention')[19] that we see the greatest mismatch between the theory of universal liberty and security and the reality of their highly selective application. But the situation appears both more general and, with the return of Vladimir Putin to the presidency, to be getting worse.[20]

What marks Russia out from the pseudo-democracies is its engagement with external criticism. The reports of various international and regional bodies, as well as the interventions of political leaders from other countries, are however invariably met with defensive explanations which are strongly rooted in – as one Russian response put it to a recent visit from the Council of Europe's Commissioner for Human Rights Thomas Hammarberg – 'the fight against terrorism'. The various measures impugned by outside observers are in fact 'aimed at struggling against terrorism'. So far as the North Caucasus is concerned, 'the situation . . . in total is characterized by the continuing menace of terrorism manifestations on behalf of the active part of the illegal armed gangs acting in the region.'[21]

Similar language was used during earlier Chechnya wars (not too strong a word to use) and is regularly deployed to explain the crackdowns across the Russian republic. As the President Vladimir Putin said to US interviewer Barbara Walters in an interview shortly after the 11 September attacks, '[w]e have a common enemy, international terrorism, and the work that we are pursuing together is in our best interests'. President Putin 'understood the feelings that the Americans were feeling at that time' because of his country's own experience of terrorism and, as he said 'I'm not just referring to the Chechyna and the Caucasus'.[22] When addressing a meeting of the National Anti-Terrorism Committee held in Vladikavkaz on 22 February 2011, the then Russian Federation President Dmitry Medvedev stated that '[i]t is here that our citizens are faced with terror on a daily basis. Terror exists in other parts of our country too, but in the North Caucasus it is present almost everywhere, and terrorist attacks occur quite regularly, unfortunately.'[23] As one recent news analysis remarked, 'the idea of a global war on terrorism remains one of Putin's key political narratives. It is trotted out to this day after every terrorist attack in the Russian heartland and during most discussions with Western leaders, who see it as a firm bond in their alliances with Moscow.'[24]

The route in to this has taken different legal shapes down the years but is now to be found via Federal Law No 35-FZ, adopted by the State Duma on 26 February 2006 and endorsed by the Federation Council on 1 March 2006. Article 3 defines terrorism as 'the ideology of violence and the practice of influencing the adoption of a decision by public authorities, local self-government bodies or international organizations connected with frightening the population and (or) other forms of unlawful violent actions.' Terrorist activity is taken to mean

> activity including the following: (a) arranging, planning, preparing, financing and implementing an act of terrorism; (b) instigation of an act of terrorism; (c) establishment of an unlawful armed unit, criminal association (criminal organization) or an organized group for implementation of an act of terrorism, as well as participation in such structure; (d) recruiting, arming, training and using terrorists; (e) informational or other assistance to planning, preparing or implementing an act of terrorism; (f) popularization of terrorist ideas, dissemination of materials or information urging terrorist activities, substantiating or justifying the necessity of the exercise of such activity.

A 'terrorist act' is constituted by

> making an explosion, arson or other actions connected with frightening the population and posing the danger of loss of life, of causing considerable damage to property or the onset of an ecological catastrophe , as well as other especially grave consequences, for the purpose of unlawful influence upon adoption of a decision by public authorities, local self government bodies or international organizations, as well as the threat of committing the said actions for the same purpose.

Article 6 'Using Armed Forces of the Russian Federation in the Struggle against Terrorism' bears full quotation:

> In the struggle against terrorism the Armed Forces of the Russian Federation may be used for the following: (1) preventing flights of aircrafts used for committing an act of terrorism or occupied by terrorists; (2) suppressing acts of terrorism in the inland waters and in the territorial sea of the

Russian Federation, at the seaside facilities used for industrial activities which are located on the continental shelf of the Russian Federation, as well as for ensuring safe national maritime traffic; (3) participating in a anti-terrorist operation in accordance with the procedure provided for by this Federal Law; (4) suppressing international terrorist activities outside the Russian Federation.

There is much more in a similar vein.[25]

The language of terrorism performs an important dual role here, as rhetorical cover for a government under attack for its human rights record and also as a strong legal basis for the continuation of the old habits of an authoritarian political culture that has chosen to work within the contemporary language of democracy, human rights and the rule of law. Reading through this kind of law, the difference between Russia and the pseudo- and neo-democracies may be hard to spot, and certainly there is a fellow-feeling between such states so far as counter-terrorism is concerned. As one example, on 27 March 2012, the Shanghai Cooperation Organization decided via its Regional Anti-Terrorist Structure (composed of Russia with Kazakhstan, China, Tajikistan, Uzbekistan and Kyrgyzstan) to establish a panel of border experts in countering terrorism, separatism and extremism. The same meeting also discussed further measures to counteract financing of terrorism and the use of the internet for diffusing terrorist, extremist or separatist views. It is unlikely that 'respect for human rights' was high on the agenda.

So which is the real Russia, the European member of the Council of Europe or the state at home in the company of these authoritarian partners? In a neo-democracy you can be both. In Russia it has worked so far because for a substantial portion of the population life is experienced as freer and more secure than it ever was in the past. As the Foreign Office comment quoted earlier remarked, 'human rights have improved significantly' since Soviet times, but while this may be true for some it cannot be the case for all – particularly for those who no longer have state-supported access to their basic needs and for those as well whose inclination it is to work for a genuine democracy or a properly free press or an independent rule of law. Indeed while many of the first category die through what in Soviet times would have been called culpable state neglect,[26] some at least of the latter are murdered by the state, with such killings being naturally dressed up as counter-terrorist operations.[27]

Now it is clear – and here is an important difference from the pseudo-democracies – that the engagement of Russia with external organizations means that its conduct is subject to critical scrutiny. I have mentioned already the comments of the Council of Europe's Commissioner for Human Rights Thomas Hammarberg, a regular visitor to the country, as was his predecessor Álvaro Gil-Robles.[28] There are similar interactions with UN institutional and treaty bodies, such as the High Commissioner for Human Rights Navi Pillay; Ms Pillay said at the conclusion of a six-day visit to Russia in February 2011 (in which she met the President and many other senior officials) that 'Accountability for those in power is essential, if abuse of power is to be diminished, and public trust established' and that this 'principle must be applied, and be seen to be applied, to the most senior government, state and judicial officials, and on down the entire line of command to the local administrators and the policemen and military officers in the towns and villages'.[29] In the same set of remarks the High Commissioner refers to the fact that Russia has generated the greatest backlog of cases before the European Court of Human Rights, and it is certainly true that every now and again these applications produce results. Thus we find a ruling on 20 December 2011 that the state had violated the right to life of the victims of the 2002 hostage-taking in the Dubrovka theatre in Moscow in 23–26 October 2002 by Chechen terrorists by failing to abide by their positive obligations under article 2 of the European Convention on Human Rights due to a flawed rescue plan.[30] Another example is the decision (on 28 February 2012) that the authorities had violated the right to life of the Chechen Abdula Edilov by subjecting him to an enforced disappearance and by failing to conduct effective investigations, the operation having been carried out by state agents on 26 August 2001 in an unacknowledged security operation. The Court also found a violation of the prohibition of torture and inhuman and degrading treatment for the suffering of his mother caused by the enforced disappearance of her son, and a breach of her right to an effective remedy.[31]

Do these various visits and court rulings make any difference? They must obviously do so at a certain level. The Russian authorities engage intently with each process. They have created large-scale human rights structures on the ground to make credible a commitment to human rights and the rule of law that they appreciate is regarded with some scepticism by outside observers: on her visit to Russia High Commissioner Pillay met the Federal Commissioner for Human Rights, Vladimir Lukin, and no fewer than 50 regional Commissioners for Human Rights. There are all the visits by the Council of Europe's commissioner as well. But none of this prevents the country from continuing with its hostile action against domestic dissent, from waging internal war against separatist elements within its jurisdiction and – even – invading a fellow Council of Europe member (as occurred in 2008 when Russia attacked Georgia in a dispute over South Ossetia). The two positions are held in tension, with the authorities knowing that the rejection of human rights, democracy and the rule of law that routinely (and with their connivance) occurs on the ground must not be allowed to become so extreme that the cordial engagement with external invigilators becomes too self-evidently fatuous to be able to continue with any kind of credibility. The visitors play their part in this dance, engaging, criticizing, perhaps even (in private) despairing – but not walking away. Vital to the successful managing of this tension is that the authorities have the broad support of large parts of the population, that liberty and security are experienced as real by the many for whom the oppressed few belong in an entirely separate universe, a world of 'terrorists' which they can only experience as victims and in relation to which therefore they reliably support their government in its effort at confrontation. Hobbes applies here as much as we saw him applying in twentieth-century Britain when we looked closely at his legacy in Chapter 2.

I have been talking here so far about Russia but I could nearly as easily have been referring to Turkey, or any one of a number of such states which have embraced the form and some of the content of democracy while at the same time leaving a substantial minority of their peoples (often distinguishable by their ethnic or social or economic or other status) without the guarantees of liberty and security that are enjoyed by the majority. Like Russia, Turkey commits to human rights and is a member of the Council of Europe, subscribing therefore to the European Convention on Human Rights. Like its neighbour to the north, it permits external scrutiny and engages with the monitors and observers and the human rights trainers that come from the West. But all the while it has a military side to its activities (primarily but not exclusively operating against Kurdish activists) that seems to play by entirely different rules, and it is supported in so doing by the machinery of justice. Among the relevant Turkish anti-terrorism laws are the offences of 'announcing that the crimes of a terrorist organization are aimed at certain persons', 'printing or publishing leaflets and declarations of terrorist organizations', and 'making propaganda for a terrorist organization'. On 20 December 2011, an Istanbul court ordered the arrest of 40 journalists, who were later accused of membership of the Union of Kurdistan Communities (KCK), a group allegedly linked to the banned Kurdistan Workers Party (PKK).[32] On 1 November 2011, the Istanbul 14th High Criminal Court oversaw the arrest of a publisher (Ragip Zarakolu) and an academic (Büşra Ersanlı) on charges of membership of the Turkish Assembly of the Union of Kurdistan Communities, an illegal association allegedly connected with the PKK. According to Human Rights Watch, the detentions marked 'a new low in the misuse of terrorism laws to crush freedom of expression and association in Turkey'.[33]

The judgments against the country before the European Court of Human Rights have come just as thick and fast as they have against Russia, involving but going beyond the rights of journalists relating to political speech. On 17 January 2012, for example, it was held that the right to a fair trial of one Mehmet Fídancı had been violated by Turkish authorities, after he had been arrested in April 2001 on suspicion of being a member of Hizbullah and convicted in 2009 of being part of a group which had carried out a terrorist attack, killing seven people and injuring two.[34] There are several cases dealing with the infringement by Turkish military forces of the right to life, some with harrowing facts.[35] Towards the end of 2011 the Court found the anti-terrorism authorities to have acted so brutally in suppressing a demonstration in support of PKK leader Abdullah Öcalan that they were prepared to make the highly unusual finding of a breach of article 3 (the prohibition on torture and inhuman and degrading treatment) arising out of the event.[36] The UN and regional visits from the human rights monitors continue, confirming an engagement that is all too frequently mocked by facts on the ground.[37]

## The New Normal

Both Russia and Turkey have substantial ethnic minority problems and it is in the context of dealing aggressively with the unrest generated by such situations that anti-terrorism laws invariably come into their own. In such situations the majority of the people – not from suspected ethnic backgrounds – can continue to experience liberty in a way that is entirely unaffected by any potential insecurity that hypothetically might arise from the enactment of sweeping national security laws: as with the UN blacklists from the last chapter and the UK and US laws coming up in the next, they are for other people.

The point goes beyond ethnic difference alone and embraces many more than these two countries. In a report he did for the United Kingdom in March 2007, Britain's then Independent Reviewer of Terrorism Legislation, Lord Carlile of Berriew QC, set out in tabular form a set of general descriptions of the terrorism laws of a vast number of countries – 60 in all.[38] It makes depressing reading, with broad definitions being reported across a range of these states, from older post-colonial democracies like India and Algeria through to many nations that have re-established themselves as independent in the aftermath of 1989. This works through into incidents on the ground in a thoroughly predictable fashion. There is the example of the thirteen suspected terrorists held in indefinite detention under Malaysia's Internal Security Act in November 2011, despite recent government promises to repeal the law.[39] In another state highlighted by Carlile as having a broad definition, India, the UN Special Rapporteur on extrajudicial, summary or arbitrary executions, Christof Heyns has recently called on the Government to take measures to tackle impunity in cases of extrajudicial executions, finding that 'in the North Eastern States, and Jammu and Kashmir the armed forces have wide powers to employ lethal force' with instances of extrajudicial killings having been recorded in the last years in what have been (inevitably) characterized as anti-terrorism operations against Maoist rebels or Kashmiri separatists.[40] But in a well-used formula that marks out the neo-democratic state, Heyns 'praised the openness and willingness of the Government of India to engage, shown also by the fact that it was willing to host a mission dealing with the right to life, an area in which issues to be tackled are often complex in various countries'.[41] Sometimes, as with Russia and Turkey, it seems as though the possibility of external scrutiny – a willingness to be found out – is thought in some way to dilute the severity of state coercion.

The story is similar in Africa: in Uganda, an Amnesty report at the end of 2011 detailing how anti-terrorism laws are being used to stifle dissent;[42] in Kenya, a blind man reportedly arrested on suspicion of terrorist activities and later found dead;[43] in Rwanda, the opposition leader Victoire Ingabire (facing terrorist-related charges arising out of alleged connections with a mainly ethnic Hutu group designated terrorist under local law) announcing a boycott of her trial, alleging bias on the part of the presiding judge;[44] in Algeria in January 2012, the UN Human Rights Committee issuing two decisions on the cases of enforced disappearance of Djamel and Mourad Chihoub, and of Kamel Djebrouni, finding violations of their right to life, their right not to be subject to torture or cruel, inhuman or degrading treatment in light of their incommunicado detention, their right to humane treatment in detention, their right to recognition as persons before the law, and (for Chihoub) his entitlement to special protection as a child (he was fifteen when apprehended by Algerian forces).[45] In an echo of Russia's action against Georgia, on 15 October, the Kenyan government even invoked Kenya's right to self-defence against terrorism under Article 51 of the UN Charter to justify the entry of its forces into Somalia to pursue and fight the Islamist force controlling a substantial part of the country.[46]

## International Pressure

And what of the Security Council's CTC during this explosion of anti-terrorism law and arbitrary police and military action? As we have already seen, it got going in the weeks after the attacks of 11 September and quickly grew an executive offshoot, the Counter-Terrorism Committee Executive Directorate (CTED).[47] The early years were marked by a near-disregard for the requirements of human rights but over time things have changed. As this machinery of counter-terrorism has bedded down, so we have seen a process similar to that which (as we saw in Chapter 3) gradually disciplined the work of the blacklisting committees, with something of a human rights/rule of law perspective being imposed on what had gone before. The resolution establishing the CTED (in March 2004) had mentioned the importance of international human rights law and the integration of the two fields received a further boost with the publication in 2006 of the UN's Global Counter-Terrorist Strategy.[48] Building on the work of a 'world summit' the year before, this strategy committed the UN to effective action against terrorism in a way which was henceforth explicitly to engage international human rights. Indeed the fourth of the four main heads in the 'Plan of Action' of the strategy declared nothing less than that '[m]easures to ensure respect for human rights for all and the rule of law' were '*the* fundamental basis of the fight against terrorism'.[49]

There can be little doubt that this idea of human rights protection has now reached deeply into the language of counter-terrorism. At an event celebrating the CTC's tenth anniversary, in New York in September 2011, the CTED's executive director Mike Smith acknowledged that in the years since 2006 the CTED had grown to 'recognize the importance of emphasizing . . . that human rights and counter-terrorism are mutually reinforcing and need not conflict'.[50] Indeed going even further and referring to remarks made at the same event by the CTC chair, Indian Ambassador Hardeep Singh Puri, Smith suggested that 'counter-terrorism programs that ignore the human rights dimension are less effective and can even be counter-productive'.[51] This was of a piece with the Secretary-General Ban Ki-moon's own comments, opening the event, which had among other points stressed that the CTC's 'continued focus on ensuring national respect for human rights and the rule of law [was] of great importance'.[52] A Counter-Terrorism Implementation Task Force has now been set up, with a UN Centre on Counter-Terrorism established within it, and both of these take their cue from the UN's ostensible (and certainly now loudly and frequently proclaimed) commitment to human-rights-sensitive counter-terrorism; at one meeting organized by the Secretary General and the task force which was attended by over 500 participants, the note of the event observed that '[p]articipants [had] repeatedly underlined the importance of promoting and protecting human rights and the rule of law in all counter-terrorism activities'.

Perhaps we should pause just for a moment. Is there a little bit of anxiety here in the use of the word 'repeatedly' in this summary of the meeting? That event took place as recently as 19 September 2011, in other words almost five years to the day since the global strategy was supposed to have put human rights at the centre of the UN's counter-terrorism work. Perhaps a clue to the strains to be found under the surface lies in the guest list of those speaking at this jointly hosted event. Chaired by the Ambassador from Qatar, the main speakers included the President of Krygyz-stan, and the ministers or deputy ministers for foreign affairs from (among other states) Indonesia, Saudi Arabia, Egypt, Pakistan and (unsurprisingly) Turkey and Russia. Of course there was a session devoted to 'promoting human rights and the rule of law while countering terrorism', chaired by UN High Commissioner for Human Rights Pillay, but the speak-ers who put themselves forward for this slot were from Switzerland, Norway and Botswana.[53]

While the UN counter-juggernaut does make all these references to human rights, and to that extent progress has been made, the real passion is clearly reserved for the threat posed by terrorism. To Ban Ki-moon, speaking at this 2011 meeting, 'Terrorism is still as potent a threat today as it was ten years ago' and so 'no effort' is to be 'spared to strengthen international action against this global peril'.[54] Ambassador Puri may say a few things about human rights but at the same time he declares himself 'happy to report that the inter-national community has vigorously responded to the call to rise up to the unprecedented challenges posed by terror-ism'.[55] In the eyes of the UN diplomats, terrorism appears as a kind of virus, a sort of militant bird flu capable of striking at any moment; as Puri puts it '[t]oday, terrorists are not only truly globalized, but are also waging an asymmetric warfare against the international community. . . . There is hardly any region of the world that has not been scarred by terrorism during the past decade.'[56] Joining in with the rhetoric, for all his commitment to human rights, executive director Smith cannot help but refer to terrorism as 'one of the scourges of our age . . . a phenomenon that can strike anywhere in the world with devastating impact'.[57] Echoing a phrase used by Puri in his remarks of welcome, the 'outcome document' issued after the 10th anniversary meeting urged all member states 'to ensure zero-tolerance towards terrorism'.[58] Long forgotten in all this hyped-up talk is the lack of any international consensus on what terrorism means, with even the relative discipline of speaking only of 'terrorist acts' (which are as we have seen in Chapter 3 defined internationally) having fallen by the wayside.

We know already that many states do not need to be asked twice to deploy their security forces against the few in order to support the liberty of the many – and for countries organized along democratic lines (real, pseudo or neo), cracking down on the opposition in a way that can be packaged as counter-terrorism allows government and citizens alike to see these actions as those of a free Republic preserving itself against the other rather than an ordinary authoritarian regime intent on minding its back. Depressing evidence of the central focus of the CTC in the years since 2001 can be seen in its reports on its impact in member states. The most comprehensive of these appears as an annex to a letter from Ambassador Puri to the UN Secretary-General, issued to mark the tenth anniversary of the establishment of the CTC.[59] The text is divided into 'regions and sub-regions, and draws conclusions about progress in the implementation of [resolution 1373] in key thematic areas' with '[g]aps in the implementation' of the resolution being 'identified and new practical ways to implement the resolution [being] proposed'.[60]

Positive developments are presented solely on the basis of their likely counter-terrorist efficacy, and (for all the rhetoric suggesting otherwise in the set-piece speeches) human rights when they are mentioned in the main text come across more as an obstacle to rather than a vital ingredient of that success. Thus the need to control the internet is 'necessarily constrained' by a commitment to freedom of expression ('a cornerstone of international human rights law') despite which however the UN requires action 'to suppress terrorist recruitment' and 'to prohibit and prevent incitement to commit acts of terrorism', so that in the view of the CTED (which drafted the impact survey) '[t]hese issues will continue to pose challenges in the years to come'.[61] Nor is any effort made to assess the democratic (or otherwise) credentials of the states being considered – that is for other bodies; '[i]n virtually all regions, States continue to face challenges in ensuring the compliance of their counter-terrorism measures with all their obligations under international law, including international human rights law, refugee and humanitarian law'.[62] Occupying the last three pages of this 89-page impact survey, an afterthought to the main action, is where the fact of 'serious human rights concerns in the counter-terrorism context' that 'persist in all parts of the world'[63] is given a minor walk-on part, a positioning that it might be forgivably thought neatly captures the true position of human rights in this committee's endeavours.

## Uncertain Futures

Now it could well be said that at least the CTC is asking the right sorts of questions, and that its movement is towards a greater feel for liberty and that we should acknowledge this. Recalling our earlier discussion of specific countries – Russia, Turkey and so on – it might even be said that what matters is the direction of travel of a political culture, not where a country or international organization is at a specific moment but where it is hoping to go. On this test, it might be said that these countries are all moving steadily (under the benign guidance of the CTC) towards the embracing of a true democratic style of governance and that while there are bound to be blips along the way, these blips should not be misunderstood as insuperable barriers to a better future. But this assumes that there is a terminal, unvarying and secure, marked 'true liberty and security' towards which newly emerging democracies are inexorably moving, in other words that there are these ethical tracks along which the train of such states (together with their retinue) cannot help but move.

This is a false assumption. What we think of as a real or authentic or true democracy varies over time: once it was thought that no representative element was required at all and that only a small fraction of the community could participate; later it was believed that democracy could be constituted by the male gender to the exclusion of the female; even today in supposedly established democracies we have no difficulty in reconciling this political description of where we live with the continued disenfranchisement of prisoners and young persons between the ages of sixteen and eighteen. The reason why the CTC can confidently invoke human rights in the way that it does is not because it is dishonest or indulging itself in some conscious charade. The content given to 'human rights' and the 'rule of law' and even (in some extreme cases) the meaning accorded to democracy itself, is changing in the well-established, or settled, or mature or (if we want) 'real' democracies. The movement is not only that of the new democracies towards neo-democracy, it is also of the old democracies towards neo-democracy as well. They seem to be meeting in the middle with the UN already entrenched in that space. This bleak conjunction, or (to use a dangerous liberal nostrum) this new overlapping consensus has serious consequences for universal liberty and security. It is to the downward drift of the old democracies that we now turn.

# 5

# A Very Partial Freedom

## An American Dream

On 20 January 2005, George W. Bush marked his inauguration as US president for a second term with the traditional speech after the swearing-in ceremony. His first term of office had seen a series of military engagements abroad and (as we shall see) continuing controversy at home about the erosion of civil liberties that had occurred in the aftermath of the attacks of 11 September and the government's reaction to these. Disliked intensely by many, he was nevertheless popular with enough of the electorate to secure a second mandate without the balloting controversies that had accompanied his first.

Far from running from issues of liberty and security, the speech he delivered at this moment of his greatest triumph revelled in the 'durable wisdom of our constitution'. The America which for fifty years had 'defended our own freedom by standing watch on distant borders' now needed to look for inspiration to fight both at home and abroad: there was 'only one force of history that can break the reign of hatred and resentment, and expose the pretensions of tyrants, and reward the hopes of the decent and tolerant, and that is the force of human freedom'. There is a 'moral choice between oppression, which is always wrong, and freedom, which is eternally right'. The 'survival of liberty in our land increasingly depends on the success of liberty in other lands' with 'the best hope for peace in our world' being 'the expansion of freedom in all the world'. It has become 'the urgent requirement of our nation's security, and the calling of our time' to match the proclamations of those past leaders who from 'the day of our Founding . . . have proclaimed that every man and woman on this earth has rights, and dignity, and matchless value' and in doing so 'our goal is to help others find their own voice, attain their own freedom, and make their own way'. To the doubters the President had this to say:

> Some, I know, have questioned the global appeal of liberty – though this time in history, four decades defined by the swiftest advance of freedom ever seen, is an odd time for doubt. Americans, of all people, should never be surprised by the power of our ideals. Eventually, the call of freedom comes to every mind and every soul. We do not accept the existence of permanent tyranny because we do not accept the possibility of permanent slavery. Liberty will come to those who love it.[1]

This powerful rhetoric appears bizarre to those who know of the negative impact of this president's policies on the liberty of many within his country and on the security of even more without. When he quotes former president Abraham Lincoln to the effect that '[t]hose who deny freedom to others deserve it not for themselves; and, under the rule of a just God, cannot long retain it', the sceptic wonders whether Bush himself should not be first in line for the punishment that he would mete out to others. How can appeals to freedom abroad be so confidently underpinned by such easy assumptions about liberty at home, especially at a time of such extraordinary crackdowns on dissent? But even to put the question in this way is to misunderstand the audience at which President Bush was directing his words, and is also greatly to underestimate their power.

We need at this juncture to recall our discussion of Hobbes in Chapter 2. The majority of Americans experience life as free and no end of critical engagement – or even facts on the ground – appears able to dislodge this collective of confident self-understandings. The freedom of the many is not affected or likely to be affected by government responses to terrorism – whatever Leviathan does in this regard will hardly trespass into their world – but (and this is not a foolish thought, or the result of some effective albeit subtle propaganda campaign) such liberty is vulnerable to terrorist attack. The 11 September attacks did happen after all and robust executive action to increase security is accordingly to be supported – especially as it comes with no trade-off so far as the liberty of the many is concerned. In the language of this book, Bush's presidency worked because it opened up a credible if under-articulated space within the umbrella of a broader universalistic language: 'I may seem to be talking about liberty and security for everyone, but you know and I know that I really mean you, and you know also that when I talk about counter-terrorism actions to preserve security I don't mean you.' The message is subtle but not new, having been honed during a Cold War that required similar levels of universalist rhetoric matched by even harsher actions on the ground against the 'enemy within'.[2] And it worked for George Bush right to the end, with an unpopular war and economic collapse rather than his terrorism policies bringing about his sharp decline into unpopularity.[3]

## Commander-in-Chief

So what then were the actions that President Bush took which rendered his presidency so controversial, albeit in the way that I have just described in this arena at least also so consistently well supported? And have the decisions that were taken during his eight years survived his presidency to become given features of liberty and security in contemporary America?

The very first reaction by the Administration to the attacks of 11 September was to characterize the response that was required in war terms. Within a week the president was warning that 'we're at war. There's been an act of war declared upon America by terrorists and we will respond accordingly' and that we will 'do what it takes to win'.[4] This was not just an exercise in rhetoric: the declaration of war (albeit on an emotion – terror – rather than a tangible enemy) meant that the president could unlock powers that would otherwise not have been available to him: this was Leviathan *in extremis*, the republic threatened existentially, in the words of the early twentieth century judge that we encountered in Chapter 2, *salus populi suprema lex.*[5]

Clearly and most obviously, this involved an aggressive response abroad, with the action against Afghanistan being launched shortly afterwards. Military force had been used before against violent foreign action deemed to be 'terrorist' – the capturing of those responsible for the *Achille Lauro* hijacking in 1985; the bombings of Libya in 1986; missiles launched in response to attacks on US embassies abroad – but the engagement with Afghanistan was obviously on an entirely different scale. It was sanctioned by an authorization of military force agreed by Congress three days after the 11 September attacks. This was far broader than merely permitting this action, with it also approving strikes against not only nations but groups and persons as well, just so long as this could be said to be 'in order to prevent any future acts of international terrorism against the United States by such nations, organizations or persons'.[6] Here is the original source of much of what critics have called the lawlessness of the Bush presidency on the world stage – not only the invasion of Afghanistan but the subsequent detention of suspects at military bases around the world (including at Guantanamo Bay) until the end of 'the war' and the targeted assassinations that have become if not perhaps a routine then certainly a notorious feature of US policy.

And to answer one of the questions posed a moment ago, both policies have survived relatively unscathed the departure of President Bush from office. As we shall see shortly, the Obama administration has resiled from its pledge to close Guantánamo Bay, instead surrounding its detention without charge with the sorts of spurious trappings of legality that we observed in the last chapter to be such a characteristic feature of those countries aspiring to the appearance (but without the substance) of the rule of law, what we have been calling here the neo-democracies. There has been no similar level of embarrassment or pretence, however, about extra-judicial and extra-territorial killings: these have included not only Osama bin Laden but also the US citizen Anwar al-Awlaki in Yemen in 2011. The latter action was defended by US Attorney General Eric Holder as necessary to the security of the country. Assassination was a 'loaded term' which did not apply here. Moreover, 'the American people can be – and deserve to be – assured that actions taken in their defense are consistent with their values and their laws'. Looking at this particular American's name no doubt most Americans agreed.[7]

But how far should one take such actions? Eric Holder's speech referred to 'people currently plotting to murder Americans' who reside not only 'in distant countries' but 'within our own borders as well'. Killing within the country itself may be a step too far but in the immediate aftermath of the 11 September attacks, President Bush construed his 'commander-in-chief' status as permitting him to authorize an array of extra-legal activities that in the absence of the 'war on terror' label would have been more Nixon's Watergate than Roosevelt's World War Two. A highly secret executive order authorized the National Security Agency to intercept telephone calls and emails involving suspected foreign terrorists even where this necessarily entailed listening to a side of the conversation emanating from within the United States. When the *New York Times* revealed the existence of the eavesdropping programme, it was initially defended by Administration lawyer John Yoo as something that was legitimized under the inherent power of the president (to do what he or she wants), with later apologists pointing to the congressional authorization of 14 September.[8]

The 'Commander-in-Chief' route and the Congressional authorization were not the only pathways to the robust outcomes sought by the Bush team. Deploying pre-existing legal regimes, the authorities embarked on a systematic enforcement of immigration law so rigorous that visitors risked detention where they had overstayed by as little as a day. The facts are not entirely clear but it has been estimated that more than 5,000 foreign nationals were detained in the two years after the 2001 attacks.[9] Some of those held were kept for very long periods and there were also bouts of prolonged solitary confinement, and incidents of abuse. Almost from the start the system drew severe complaints from the Office of the Inspector General.[10]

Another ruse was the use of material witness warrants which allowed the authorities to hold persons suspected of terrorism without having to arrest them on suspicion of terrorism offences (and thereby attracting the usual criminal law safeguards). The explanation for the detention was that testimony before a grand jury was pending but the effect of the law's operation made it pretty well indistinguishable from internment. In his excellent book *The 9/11 Effect*, Kent Roach has good examples of how the law worked: Osama Awadallah, suspected of a connection with the 11 September bombers, held for 83 days in solitary confinement, shackled, strip searched, and interrogated at length;[11] Jose Padilla held for a month as a material witness before being declared an enemy combatant and transferred to military custody; Brandon Mayfield held for two weeks not because of anything related to the 11 September attacks but because he was wrongly suspected of the Madrid bombings in 2004. And so on. As the last of these names suggests, the power was available against Americans as well as non-Americans, though it attracted little critical attention, not only because its transformation into an anti-terrorism power had taken place by stealth but also because (as suggested a little earlier when reflecting on President Bush's second inaugural address) 'ordinary' Americans believed in their hearts that it was nothing to do with them. They did not have foreign names and were unlikely to be unlucky enough to be another Brandon Mayfield: in any event he had converted to Islam after all and upon his release identified this as the reason for his detention, a claim denied by the FBI (although the federal government afterwards paid him $2m by way of damages for how he had been treated).[12]

## Turning to the Law

The Patriot Act differed from these various supra-legal devices and redeployments of pre-existing legal frameworks: it drew controversy precisely because it was a proper piece of law, done openly in a way that suggested that the constitution still mattered. The Hobbesian/republican principle *salus populi suprema lex* sought to drive all before it here too. For evidence we need look no further than the title: the USA Patriot Act, or – in full – the Uniting and Strengthening America by Providing Appropriate Tools Required to Intercept and Obstruct Terrorism. The legislation did not quite deliver on the promise of such dramatic language. It is true that extensive amendments were made to the Foreign Intelligence Surveillance Act 1978 (FISA), expanding the grounds on which actions to secure such intelligence could be permitted and permitting searches of a wider range of potential sources than would earlier have been allowed. Further amendments to the same Act also permitted the deployment of this kind of intelligence in the context of local law enforcement. Other provisions in the Patriot Act gave law enforcement officials wider powers to secure evidence related to terrorism investigations from third parties. There were sections devoted to implementing UN Security resolution 1373 which as we saw in Chapter 3 was the main vehicle for the galvanizing of international opinion against terrorism. There was a decent and on the whole relatively restrained effort at the definition of terrorism.[13]

Looking back, the Act does not seem to justify the furore it created at the time, especially when read in light of the other counter-terrorism powers of which the Bush Administration was then covertly availing itself. The strong hostility

shown it by civil society came from both traditionally progressive civil libertarian groups and also the more conserva-
tively inclined libertarians. In the years after its enactment,
judges revealed their own distaste in cases in which they
either gave the measure a restricted interpretation or even
ruled parts of it unconstitutional.[14] Such critical engagement
is not surprising: this is exactly the sort of opposition that is
created if a measure of this kind appears genuinely universal
– the moment those who take their freedom for granted see
a real threat to their particular circumstance in proposed
legislation is bound to be a point of danger for that legislation. It was because the president did not get all he wanted
from the Patriot Act that he found himself tempted into the
supra- or barely legal eavesdropping that we discussed earlier.
Americans saw more potential for the legislation reaching
the un-Islamic Brandon Mayfield Americans as well as the
un-American Americans like Osama Awadallah, Anwar
al-Aulaqi and Jose Padilla.

The last of these names is an important part of America's
liberty and security story for a reason apart from his brief
encounter with the authorities as a material witness. As
mentioned earlier, and also of course notoriously, one of the
major initiatives of the Bush administration had been to
create detention camps around the world, out of the reach
of US law and therefore (or so it was assumed) capable of
functioning with impunity as holding centres for people held
without charge on suspicion of their involvement as 'enemy
combatants' or as 'unlawful combatants' in the 'war on
terror'. Widely regarded as black holes into which no form
of law could enter, it was from a number of these environ-
ments (notably Bagram Theater Internment Facility and Abu
Ghraib prison, both in Iraq) that horrific stories of torture
and ill-treatment of detainees began to emerge. Terrible
though the abuse was, the impact of these revelations on
Americans was doubly vicarious: it was happening not to
them, and not to people like them but to foreigners abroad.
Unlike the Patriot Act it carried no immediate resonance

along the lines of 'this could be you'. The liberty of Americans was entirely unthreatened while their security was – they were being told – improved.

It was the same for the Guantánamo Bay camp that had grown to deal with the detainees delivered to it under a military order issued by the President on 13 November 2001, on his own authority as commander in chief and by reason of the 14 September congressional authorization as well. The order provided for the detention and trial by military commission of suspected Al-Qaida operatives or others who were suspected of being involved in 'international terrorism'.[15] Though the details were not provided, it was clear that such commissions were to have a procedure markedly different from and far less rigorous than the ordinary criminal trial, despite the fact that the punishments of life imprisonment and death were specifically stated to be within the range of penalties they were empowered to impose.[16] The order explicitly sought to exclude any review of the activities of such commissions by US, foreign or international courts[17] and also went to some length to ensure that 'state secrets' should never be revealed as an accident of whatever the process was that finally emerged.[18] There was case-law supporting such draconian military adjudication when the nation was at war: another reason why the 'war on terror' was more than just a rhetorical flourish.[19]

Clearly this facility was designed for foreigners. Because of this, though they attracted international opprobrium and the indignation of US civil libertarians, the political cost exacted on the Administration was slight. As we have seen, President Bush's second inaugural address was able to rhapsodize about freedom without even feeling the need to explain away or justify how Guantánamo fitted in such a story. The 13 November Order specifically excluded Americans from its remit but it was only a matter of time before such a case would test the system that it had put in place. This is where Jose Padilla comes back into the picture. Shortly before his one-month detention as a material witness was to be made the subject of a judicial review, a presidential order (issued in June 2002) required that he be detained as an enemy combatant (due to his association, it was said, with Al-Qaida). Guantánamo not being available as he was a US citizen, he was moved to a military brig in South Carolina where he was denied access to the outside world and the (indefinite) detention that followed was marked by lengthy periods of (at the very least) 'robust' interrogation. The Supreme Court avoided the issues of principles in the case when the matter reached it, finding that the suit had been filed in the wrong state, New York instead of South Carolina where the commander of the ship (and therefore, unusually, the jailor) lived and worked.[20] What was interesting, though, was that now – nearly three years on from 11 September – only the narrowest of margins could be garnered to avoid ruling on the government's actions. One of the dissentients in the 5-4 decision, Justice Stevens, gave an early indication of how these cases might eventually go, noting that 'if this Nation is to remain true to the ideals symbolized by its flag, it must not wield the tools of tyrants even to resist an assault by the forces of tyranny'.[21]

The obstacle of democracy had restricted the breadth of the Patriot Act and now a narrow opening had been made within which the principle of the rule of law, standing outside republican necessity, might do the same. The *Padilla* case rumbled on and was about to return to the Supreme Court on the issue of whether it should be prosecuted as a criminal rather than military matter when Padilla was suddenly indicted on broad charges of terrorism (unrelated to the reasons why he had been originally detained).[22] In the case of Yaser Hamdi, an American citizen captured in Afghanistan who had been placed in Guantánamo only to be transferred to a naval brig in Virginia (and afterwards one in South Carolina) when his citizenship became known, the Supreme Court agreed that some rudimentary due process was due him, but with four of the nine justices being prepared once again to go much further than this.[23] A remarkable feature of the case is that a strong dissenting opinion by the most radically conservative member of the Court

Antonin Scalia was joined by the Court's most venerable progressive John Paul Stevens. For Scalia (and Stevens) the 'very core of liberty secured by our Anglo-Saxon system of separated powers has been freedom from indefinite imprisonment at the will of the Executive' and this had been breached by the action taken against Hamdi. On the view of these two Justices, the petitioner should have been 'entitled to a habeas decree requiring his release unless (1) criminal proceedings [were] promptly brought, or (2) Congress [had] suspended the writ of habeas corpus' – which here of course it had not. The government avoided the implications of this decision so far as Hamdi was concerned – deporting him to Saudi Arabia on condition, among other matters, that he disavow his citizenship[24] – but the momentum it had generated across the political spectrum on the Court could not be so easily banished.

In *Rasul v Bush*[25] – decided on the same day as *Hamdi v Rumsfeld* – the Supreme Court asserted jurisdiction over the detentions in Guantánamo despite the fact that the people there (including of course the petitioners in the case before them) were not American. The ruling was rooted in a narrow point of statutory interpretation and – after some more back and forth between the three branches of government[26] – eventually produced a further piece of clarificatory repression in late Autumn 2006.[27] What the democratic branch failed to secure, its judicial equivalent then imposed, in the form of a constitutional guarantee of habeas corpus unless that remedy had been set aside in the appropriate manner – something that had not happened either in the case before it or indeed generally. This Supreme Court decision, in the law reports as *Boumediene v Bush*,[28] is rightly celebrated for having 'found' in the US constitution a geographically unrestricted right to habeas corpus that had not been known hitherto to have existed, and under the American system the senior judges have in such circumstances the final say, with their version of the constitution trumping all legislative and executive alternatives. The political atmosphere surrounding the 'war on terror' which had already begun to change by the time of the earlier cases in 2004 had definitely soured by June 2008 when *Boumediene* was decided: President Bush was on his way out, and enormous damage had been done by the press revelations of torture and ill-treatment of suspects by US personnel in Abu Ghraib and other detention facilities (including Guantánamo). How big a victory for universal liberty was this decision?

## Neo-Democracy Comes to America

It is one thing to assert a right to habeas corpus, quite another to say what the government must do to meet its demands. For all that the remedy insists on is that the jailor justify the incarceration, not that the detainee be immediately given his or her liberty. The right is a procedural remedy rather than a substantive guarantee. In the months after the ruling everything was thought to hinge on the presidential election due the following November: the Democratic candidate Barack Obama seemed to offer a new deal so far as civil liberties were concerned. Thus after his victory in November 2008, and almost immediately upon assuming office the following January, it was not a great surprise that President Obama should have issued an executive order requiring that Guantánamo be closed within one year, 'consistent with the national security and foreign policy interests of the United States and the interests of justice'.[29]

The following year proved a difficult one for the Administration. After military commissions had been suspended and a strong effort made to release, try or transfer all the detainees, it became apparent (to the Administration at any rate) that some of the detainees were simply too dangerous to release while also being impossible to prosecute.[30] This being once again an era of law rather than of supra-constitutional military necessity, a new system of detention was therefore introduced, by a presidential order dated 7 March 2011.[31] The resiling from the previously clear position on Guantánamo was disguised by an overt shift to a more liberal legal regime. The 'constitutional privilege of the right of habeas corpus' was explicitly recognized[32]and periodic review of the legitimacy of each detention promised. But the test of the need for detention remained very wide, with continued incarceration being permitted if it was judged 'necessary to protect against a significant threat to the security of the United States'. In place of the old system of military commissions, a Periodic Review Board was now constituted before which each detainee would appear to have tested the necessity of his or her detention. A full review of each detention was promised every three years with a lighter 'file review' for every detainee every six months. Humane treatment was promised, a rudimentary form of appeal permitted (albeit not one that the detainee could initiate), and reviews of the whole system established. The Order also contained a vaguely expressed imperative to continue to seek criminal prosecution whenever feasible.[33]

It is true that those brought before these boards have more rights than they have had under the old regime and more too than would be enjoyed in an ordinary theatre of war. But if the analogy was to be with the mainstream criminal process, then the situation appears in a far less good light. The executive order requires that classified documentation be withheld from detainees and instead of ordinary counsel a 'personal representative' with the right security clearance is to be hired by the government to put the case on the prisoner's behalf, though even this person is not guaranteed to be given the whole story against their 'client'. And if a detainee has the temerity to instruct private counsel, then he or she could find him or herself at a serious disadvantage, the government being empowered by the order to withhold details of the case against the detainee where it determines 'that the need to protect national security, including intelligence sources and methods, or law enforcement or privilege concerns, require[d] [it] to provide counsel with a sufficient substitute or summary of the information' instead.[34]

If all this had been produced by one of the newer democracies, of the sort we discussed in the last chapter, then we can be fairly sure that it would have been castigated as empty window-dressing by NGOs around the world and perhaps even by the US itself (if the country happened to be one of those which was fair game so far as the State Department's ethics were concerned, ie not a trusted ally). With a second Military Commissions Act passed in 2009, it represents what Kent Roach has rightly characterized as a 'further legalization of the process' of promulgating the 'war on terror' as it is now not called.[35] But what kind of a legalization is it, one designed to provide basic guarantees to ensure fair play when acting with the brute force of overwhelming state power to ruin a person's life, or one intended to throw the public's conscience off the scent while achieving exactly the effect that had been sought by the cruder instruments of coercion chosen by President Bush?

The paradoxical consequence of improvement here is that it entrenches the defective whole more deeply in law and culture, making the previously unthinkable now part of the new normal, a system of indefinite administrative detention for foreigners. And why stop at foreigners? As Padilla and Hamdi have already shown there are domestic 'suspected terrorists' as well, albeit with names and ethnicities that cause those who enjoy their freedom to the full to feel unthreatened by the disasters that befall them. How much longer before these commissions spread (replete with their ersatz due process) beyond Guantánamo and into the US itself to enmesh the wrong sort of Americans within their repressive reach? To get a taste of a likely future we can look now at the UK which has made a similar journey, and is further along its very own depressingly neo-democratic path.

## Belmarsh

The United Kingdom has long had a rather inflated reputation for being the mother of all democracies and a place of guaranteed liberty for all. We saw in Chapter 2 how easily the principle of *salus populi* trumped that of *lex* so far as Communist and other leftist agitators were concerned, both before and during the Cold War. The power of internment was regularly deployed against nationalist dissenters in Northern Ireland, most recently in the early 1970s when the gross ill-treatment of certain detainees led to an important and controversial ruling against the UK by the European Court of Human Rights, secured on the application of Britain's neighbour the Republic of Ireland.[36] In 1988 a broadcasting ban was imposed on, among others, political parties advocating a strongly nationalist position in Northern Ireland – another example of the wrong kind of speech of the sort we have earlier seen exemplified in the words of a British Home Secretary a couple of generations before.[37]

Despite these sub-currents of selective repression, the country has managed consistently to present itself as a place of freedom. In a speech on liberty in October 2007, the then Prime Minister Gordon Brown spoke of 'a distinctly British interpretation of liberty – one that asserts the importance of freedom from prejudice, of rights to privacy, and of limits to the scope of arbitrary state power . . .'.[38] Like President Bush in his inaugural speech in January 2005, the UK prime minister was able to articulate these ideas without risking absurdity because the vision of liberty that he held before his audience was only apparently universal, focusing as a matter of fact (if not, it is true, rhetoric) on the freedom of the many rather than the liberty of all. This is what allowed him – as it allowed Bush – to paint a picture of liberty threatened from the outside: 'Terrorism can strike anywhere and anytime' with the 'very freedoms we have built up over generations [being] the freedoms terrorists most want to destroy.'[39] So a speech about liberty became a launch pad for a discussion about extended pre-charge detention: 'The police and others . . . have argued that the clear trends in recent terrorist cases towards greater complexity, greater numbers and international links suggest that in the future 28 days may not be enough.'[40] This is how neo-democracy works.

Even allowing ourselves some cynicism about earlier 'golden ages', the shift in conventional thinking on liberty in Great Britain has been truly remarkable. During the period when the country was enduring a serious campaign of politically motivated violence (from the IRA), the outer limit on detention without charge was no more than seven days – and this was in itself exceptional, explained only by the exigencies of a situation that the European Court of Human Rights had accepted amounted to what was (in the language of the European Convention on Human Rights) a 'public emergency threatening the life of the nation'.[41] Throughout this period a strong inhibition on executive action had been imposed via the insistence that all terrorism laws were temporary, requiring annual renewal in Parliament and occasional fresh re-enactment. The effect of this was to continue to engage elected representatives in a discussion about what terrorist violence necessitated; governments were allowed to take nothing for granted. This changed, controversially, with the enactment in 2000 (at the behest of the newly elected Labour government headed by Tony Blair) of a permanent Terrorism Act.

By then, however, the political safeguard of parliamentary oversight had been replaced by a judicial equivalent, in the form of another Labour initiative, the Human Rights Act 1998. This measure required that all legislation (including of course the terrorism laws) be read in a way that was compatible with the European Convention on Human Rights '[s]o far as it [was] possible to do'[42] this and that if it proved not possible, the senior judges were to be empowered to issue what the Act called 'declarations of incompatibility.' These unusual legal specimens were designed not to be legally enforceable in the traditional sense – judges would not be able to set aside Acts of Parliament or the actions of public servants necessitated by such measures. But the declaration would allow them to express their judicial distaste at the breach of rights involved, and of course the idea was that this would put pressure on Parliament and the government to act.

These human rights protections became immensely important in the immediate aftermath of the attacks of 11 September 2001. Though the events on that day had taken place outside the jurisdiction, Tony Blair was one of the first world leaders immediately to characterize the actions of Al-Qaida as an attack on people everywhere and not just in the USA. It followed that the world should respond, not only (as we have seen) in the form of UN action but at the national level as well. Within weeks of 11 September, the Anti-terrorism, Crime and Security bill had been introduced into the UK parliament and it passed into law on 14 December 2001. Its most controversial feature concerned the power it gave the executive to impose indefinite detention without charge on persons reasonably suspected by the Home Secretary of being 'international terrorists',[43] a move that required a fresh derogation from the European Convention on the basis that, as with Northern Ireland earlier, it was warranted by the 'public emergency' that now confronted the nation. In the course of the months following its enactment a handful of men were picked up – eight on 19 December 2001; a ninth on 5 February 2002; two in April 2002; one in October 2002; another in the following month; a few more in 2003.[44]

Now these were non-UK nationals whom it was judged the country would be well rid of, but who couldn't be expelled anywhere either because no country would take them or the countries that would (including invariably their own) would be likely to ill-treat them on their return in a way that would offend their human rights under the UK Human Rights Act. (It was by this time settled law that the Act could be used to stop the removal of people from the UK to places where there was a serious risk of death, or torture, or inhuman or degrading treatment or punishment.)[45] It might be thought that the obvious option for such unattractive characters – especially given the suspicion of terrorist activity – would be to charge and try them for one of the myriad of crimes which such persons invariably commit when engaged in violent subversive activities, offences that go well beyond substantive acts to include planning, conspiracy, and even (in Britain) possessing material for a purpose reasonably suspected of being terrorist, directing 'at any level' the activities of a terrorist organization, and much else besides.[46] However the judgment that drove the detention provisions of the 2001 Act was that there was a cohort of terrorists who were not only too unpopular to deport but also too clever to be caught committing criminal offences.

These provisions did not attract a very great deal of controversy when going through Parliament in the Autumn after the 11 September attacks and subsequently: such concern as was generated was very much from civil libertarian activists rather than the general public. Essentially the argument was broadly accepted that to maintain security the liberty of these dangerous outsiders needed to be curtailed, quite possibly for ever if the struggle against terrorism proved to be without end. One or two left the country but most remained in detention, in Belmarsh prison. In a way that anticipated President Obama's normalization of Guantánamo, there were quasi-legal proceedings put in place to provide the required semblance of due process – the government-appointed 'special advocate' to represent the detainee's interests but without being his lawyer in the normal sense; the tribunal (now re-designated a court) with the job of confirming the detention to be warranted but with none of the usual features of the criminal process (a jury; full disclosure of evidence; etc.); the promises of regular review and of access to the higher courts on points of law; and so on. The men's appeals against their predicament were all rejected, with the cases having taken over eighteen months even to get to the tribunal/court in which their defeat was collectively confirmed.[47]

If the parliamentary process had not been taxing for the authorities, then the judicial safeguards proved themselves altogether more effective. As I have already said earlier, the virtue of the idea of human rights from the point of view of the protection of liberty is the momentum it generates towards universalism: it is the 'human' that matters, not where he or she is from (or what his or her views are, or which gender he or she is – the point is a general one). In this way, again as we have already discussed,[48] a properly functioning law of human rights can play an important role in resisting the plunge in the direction of selective liberty which this book has been tracking as a key part of the drift to what we have been calling here 'neo-democratic' forms of government.

In a now famous but at the time largely unexpected ruling just before Christmas in 2004, the then most senior court in Britain (the appellate committee of the House of Lords, since superseded by the UK Supreme Court) ruled that the detentions under the 2001 Act were a breach of the right to liberty (under article 5 of the European Convention) taken together with the right to non-discrimination (article 14 of the same charter of rights), and that the actions that had been taken were not legitimate under the derogation provision (which had also been indirectly included together with the Convention rights when the Human Rights Act had been enacted and were here being relied upon by the government).[49] The judges were on the whole disinclined to question the Home Secretary's assertion about there being a state of emergency – this was thought to be a matter on which the executive's view had to be accorded great weight. But what the law lords did feel able to do – and did with rare and commendable gusto – was challenge the logic behind the incarcerations that were permitted, as opposed to those that were not. In particular, why were only foreigners vulnerable? This was a knock-out question that the government simply could not answer – the honest response (because they are outsiders and no one will make a fuss) could not be given because of the universalism of the human rights legislation, and yet the alternative – we are lucky, there are no British terrorists at all – was (even before the London bombings of July 2005) self-evidently preposterous.

The ruling of the House of Lords was not that the men go free – the 2001 Act had been too clear for that. Rather the court issued a declaration of incompatibility under the Human Rights Act. The law remained but with its nasty odour of a human rights violation now evident for all to smell. The government had a choice: it could have left the legislation just as it was or re-enacted it in identical terms, in each case citing the exigencies of national security and flaunting the label 'human rights abuser' with pride rather than hiding it with embarrassment. To its credit it did neither of these two things, introducing instead new legislation in the Spring of 2005 which replaced the disgraced detention provisions of the 2001 Act with a new system of control orders.[50] These were restrictions on the general liberty of persons which were – crucially – capable of being imposed on anyone within the jurisdiction. Their terms were potentially draconian and could be put in place without any of the safeguards that normally accompanied the imposition of what looked very much like serious criminal penalties, not detention, it is true, but pretty much everything short of this.

In a marked contrast with what had happened during the autumn of 2001, the proposed universality of these orders meant that they were extensively debated in Parliament, particularly in the upper house (the House of Lords, now in its parliamentary rather than judicial mode) where many changes to the original proposals were conceded simply in order to get the measure through. Later cases in which such orders were challenged then imposed various further requirements on the state over and above what had appeared on the face of the legislation, and once again this was done in the name of human rights, this time the right to due process. In particular, the courts insisted that there had to be a 'core irreducible minimum' of fairness before the lives of even terrorist suspects could be so brutally damaged in this way.[51] And that these orders were coercive could not be disputed: one man forced to live in an unfamiliar city in social isolation and subject to a fourteen-hour curfew;[52] a sixteen-hour curfew in another case;[53] a suspect forced to relocate from Derby to Chesterfield and then made the subject of a sixteen-hour curfew in another;[54] and an Ethiopian national required to move from London to the midlands, electronically tagged and subject to a sixteen-hour curfew.[55] And we need to recall that in none of these cases were criminal charges brought or criminal proceedings initiated: the control order process stood outside the normal law.

With the exception of the last of the examples I have just given (where the suspect was released from the control order only to be re-arrested pending deportation and then subject to an eighteen-hour curfew as part of his bail conditions), all of the control orders mentioned here were upheld in the High Court, in other words found to be compatible with the human rights entitlements of those subject to them. This is another of the ways in which 'neo-democracy' works: instead of openly rejecting the principles of democracy, the rule of law and respect for human rights, it embraces all of these fine ideas but in a hug that carries with it a strong whiff of substantive oppression for all the apparent welcome that the physical act appears to entail: the embrace of a rival mafia boss at a capo's funeral.

Not that the point should be exaggerated so far as Britain is concerned. The compulsory residency requirements of the control orders proved very unpopular and as a result of a change of government in 2010 the whole scheme was replaced with a slightly milder version, now called Terrorism Prevention and Investigation Measures (TPIMs).[56] Only 52 people (all men; all suspected of involvement in Islamic-based terrorism) were made subject to the control order regime during the six years that it was in operation, with the duration of each ranging from a few months to more than four and a half years. Significantly, whereas when the system first came in all those subject to it were foreign nationals, by the end of 2011, with the law winding down in preparation for TPIMs, all were British.[57] While the identity of those subject to control orders is kept confidential, we can be fairly sure from the way that the system is constructed that the great majority if not all of the British nationals affected in this way are both Moslem and non-white in ethnic terms.

## The Habit Spreads

The story this chapter has told is not unique to the United States and to the United Kingdom. Such 'hyper-legislation'[58] afflicts analogous democracies such as Australia, New Zealand and Canada. In the first of these countries the pace of legislation was faster than anywhere else: according to Roach no fewer than 44 different statutes between 2001 and the fall of the Howard government in 2007.[59] These included a broad definition of terrorism together with the usual spectrum of wide terrorism offences, pre-charge detention powers, control orders, and also (this unique to Australia) a new set of powers awarded its domestic security agency to detain and question suspected terrorists.[60] And so far as New Zealand is concerned, as detailed by George Williams in a recent essay,[61] a Terrorism Suppression Act passed in 2002 (and subsequently amended) has provided a vehicle for the operation of UN blacklists, with later counter-terrorism and immigration laws (complete with UK-style 'special advocates') also being deployed in ways that in all likelihood would not have been politically possible before the traumatic events of 11 September. Canada has followed the same dismal path: a broad definition of terrorism, new offences, extensive new administrative powers and administrative detention based on evidence not made available to the persons affected.[62] In one particularly shocking case, Canadian officials were found to have been complicit in the passing on of inaccurate intelligence about a Canadian citizen who was subsequently tortured by Syrian intelligence officers.[63] Thus are the emerging neo-democracies of former authoritarian states being met halfway by the decline into neo-democracy of the established democratic powers.

Of course in all these countries and many other established democracies besides, the laws that are enacted appear to have a general application. As with other periods in the past, however, it is how universal laws are applied in practice that affects how they are perceived, much more than the mere fact of their potential universality. Let me end this chapter by returning to Britain and the United States. Yes, any American could be suddenly arrested as a material witness, or thrown onto a brig in Virginia, just as any Brit could theoretically be made subject to a control order or a TPIM (just as any of them could all have been arrested for

sedition or breaches of the official secrecy legislation during
the Cold War or arrested for seven days under terrorism
legislation in the 1970s) but the 'ordinary' such person
simply won't be, and this is not because such laws apply only
to foreign nationals – as we have seen they cover home
nationals as well – but because they are *de facto* aimed at
people who are not like us, not 'real' Americans or 'true'
Brits.

In a brilliant essay in the *London Review of Books*, the
campaigning lawyer Gareth Pierce's piece on the position of
Moslems in Britain is given the heading 'Was it like this for
the Irish?'[64] While it is undoubtedly overstated to describe
the situation as involving a 'war on British Muslims', as the
*Review* does on its front cover, the fact remains that those
engaged in Islamic-based political activity or in anti-imperial
or anti-war political agitation are exceptionally vulnerable
to these laws in a way that the rest of us simply are not, but
in a way that the Irish were in relation to the legislation
designed to deal with them during the 1970s and 1980s. The
difference between the current position in the US and the UK
and the various situations we earlier described in places like
Russia and Turkey remains marked, of course, but it is one
of degree not of substance. Every now and again the wrong
national gets caught up in the anti-terrorism web, Brandon
Mayfield, for example, whose compensation for being
wrongly held came (as we have seen) to $2m. When a retired
businessman found himself being extradited from Britain to
the United States to face arms-dealing charges, he was quoted
as saying (referring to a notorious terrorist suspect) 'Abu
Qatada is walking the streets of London and we cannot
extradite him. He has more rights than I have. If I was a
terrorist I would not be going to America.'[65] Like a trio of
bankers who faced similar extradition proceedings some
years before,[66] the response is first puzzlement and then fury:
what has this law to do with me; it is for other (different)
people.

# 6

# Cultural War

## Doing the Right Thing

The beauty of representative democracy lies in the way it provides both a way of shaping society while also being able, through its agnosticism on substance, to facilitate whatever it is that the will of the people, properly constituted, wants next. Blind to outcomes but alive to the vitality of process, no better way has yet been devised of doing public good without having to force a fixed meaning on what good should entail. But there are limits. For many the idea of democracy must entail some political (and perhaps even legal) inhibition on the breach of basic human rights. Nor is it any part of democracy's excellence that it should willingly succumb to self-destruction in the name of the freedom to which it is so ostentatiously devoted. This is why even the finest representative democracy will always have a problem with untrammelled free speech.

Where words are used (on a platform; on the Internet; in print) to secure specific acts of violence for a political end, this is usually and rightly classed as crime by a democracy and punished accordingly, sometimes even as treason. Trickier is general agitation within the law whose purpose is avowedly the destruction of the democratic system itself, and its replacement by not only a fresh set of policies but a new way of making policies as well (fascism; oligarchy; a communist vanguard). As we saw in Chapter 2, organizations devoted to such transformative procedural and substantive change often find themselves disabled from doing their destructive work, either by being banned or by being so hemmed in by restrictions as to be rendered incapable of functioning.[1] The issue is a difficult one even for those who approach it in the utmost good faith: how do you weed out from among your opponents (all of whom you want to keep out) those so dangerous that they need to be restricted by the law and those who require merely to be defeated in an open political fight.[2]

It is hardly surprising that democratic leaders often confuse the two, seeing their resistance to certain kinds of disruptive radicalism as a battle between right and wrong. Certainly this was the case during the Cold War; it is what made it possible for a British Home Secretary to justify the convictions of Communist Party members (for seditious libel and incitement) as being driven by 'the real necessity of preserving the right type of freedom of speech'.[3] Such activists were free to try to change things as long as they did not use 'violent and unconstitutional' means.[4] The same elision between violence and unacceptable extremism occurred during the UK's long struggle against Irish separatist violence in the last third of the twentieth century, with one particularly controversial offshoot of this battle of ideas (mentioned in passing in the last chapter) being a media ban imposed on IRA supporters and those who shared the goals of that militantly republican organization.[5] Both of these examples show us how democratic government can allow itself to 'fight back' against those who would destroy it, crushing some freedom in order to preserve freedom or, in the now notorious phrase of one later defender of a more recent brand of coercive democracy, doing 'the lesser evil'.[6]

Where does all this fit with the central theme of this book, the tracking of the growth of neo-democracy, the term I have been using here to describe the modern tendency to see liberty as in reality a selective rather than universal entitlement and security as something that only those with liberty ought to have, even if it is at the expense of others? Now (as we have seen) the selectivity inherent in this partial approach to liberty and security needs always to be disguised, either because neo-democracy is loath to cast off its egalitarian/democratic cover entirely or (much the same thing perhaps) it finds democratic ideas too entrenched to be able easily to dispense with them. So the kind of tough actions, the 'lesser evils', that are sanctioned by the need to defend democracy against its enemies, can do temptingly good work as explanations of why the liberty of some must be truncated to preserve the security of the whole. The line can be easily adopted that if left uncontrolled, this hostile liberty will destroy us – our culture; our values; our way of life – and so it has to be resisted.

This fear had centred on Islam since well before the attacks of 11 September 2001. Dating at least from the success of the Iranian revolution in 1979, it came to the minds of many when the leader of that revolt, the Atayollah Khomeini, issued a fatwa in 1989 against the author Salman Rushdie for the perceived offence caused to Moslems by the content of one of his books. By then, as a leading writer on terrorism had already put it (making the link as early as 1986), '[t]he new wave of political violence in the Middle East and South Asia . . . in which religious sectarianism is a potent factor . . . has focussed attention sharply on the real danger to civilization and international order which epidemic terrorism could pose.'[7] The 11 September attacks gave such thinking a further huge boost. It is not just people they want to kill but civilization – our civilization – they want to destroy. And it is not just the frontline bad guys we need to stop, it is their strategists and thinkers as well. To survive, democracy and human rights needed to go muscular.

## Global Clamp-Down

The immediate response by the UN to the 11 September attacks was focused on tackling acts of terrorism as such. In its preambular remarks to Resolution 1373, the Security Council expressed itself 'deeply concerned' by the increase

. . . of acts of terrorism motivated by intolerance or extremism'.[8] The shift to a wider set of targets came only after the London bombings of July 2005. The then United Kingdom Prime Minister Tony Blair had long been willing to deploy violence for ethical ends and already had entrenched views on the need to adopt a global strategy to counter the challenge of Islamic-based terrorism. So far as the first of these was concerned, as early as April 1999 he had developed his 'doctrine of the international community' as a way of galvanizing support for an intervention in Kosovo.[9] In relation to the second, he had – in March 2004 – spoken in almost apocalyptic terms of 'Islamic extremism and terrorism' being driven 'not by a set of negotiable political demands, but by religious fanaticism.'[10] After the London bombings Mr Blair returned to this theme, promoting legislation to tackle Islamic-based speech at home (on which more shortly). Meanwhile, further afield, he 'was a key player behind the scenes at the UN Security Council in drafting Resolution 1624 and getting it passed'.[11] This intervention, dated 14 September 2005, opened a new front, against a much wider range of enemies (without and within) than had earlier been contemplated.

The shift was immediately clear from the language in the new resolution's preamble. Now it was not just 'acts of terrorism' but 'the incitement of terrorist acts' and the 'justification or glorification' of such acts that were to be condemned, on the basis that these 'may incite further terrorist acts'. The 'incitement of terrorist acts motivated by extremism and intolerance' posed 'a serious and growing danger to the enjoyment of human rights, threaten[ed] the social and economic development of all States, undermin[ed] global stability and prosperity and [had to] be addressed urgently and pro-actively by the United Nations and all States'. Accordingly it was demanded of all states that they

adopt such measures as may be necessary and appropriate and in accordance with their obligations under international law to:

(a) Prohibit by law incitement to commit a terrorist act or acts;
(b) Prevent such conduct;
(c) Deny safe haven to any persons with respect to whom there is credible and relevant information giving serious reasons for considering that they have been guilty of such conduct.[12]

Paragraph 3 of the resolution went even further, calling upon states, among other actions, 'to prevent the subversion of educational, cultural and religious institutions by terrorists and their supporters'. Responsibility for enforcement of all this was handed over to the Security Council's Counter-Terrorism Committee (CTC).[13] Now it is only fair to add that the (I am tempted to say 'usual') saving clause also appears, requiring that all this should happen in accordance with international law, 'in particular international human rights law, refugee law, and humanitarian law'.[14] This is a little reminiscent of that last section of the CTC's tenth anniversary report that we encountered in Chapter 4, the nod in the direction of old-fashioned UN values after the real work has been done.[15]

## The Opening Seized

Perhaps some newly emerging democratic states might have thought twice about taking up the UN's invitation to crack down on domestic dissent as incitements to terrorism for fear of drawing negative publicity from human rights NGOs and (particularly) the governments of the established democracies of the global North. If they did, it cannot have been for long: these supposedly securely entrenched democracies were themselves among the quickest off the blocks to show that a wide range of the wrong kinds of speech were now no longer to be tolerated. The Council of Europe had already anticipated the UN, with the Convention on the Prevention of Terrorism that it opened for signature in May 2005 containing a clause purporting to clamp down on the 'public

provocation' of terrorist offences.[16] And as already foreshadowed, an early response to resolution 1624 was immediately
forthcoming from the UK.

As a main purveyor of a 'battle of civilizations'
approach,[17] it was not surprising that Tony Blair's government should have speedily submitted a draft Bill to Parliament. In its very earliest forms, this proposed measure had
appeared to involve the Home Secretary in the job of creating
a list of historical 'terrorist' events which under the new
regime it would then be a crime to glorify (any Hezbollah
victory over Israel; a successful attack against Western forces)
and others which would be exempted (e.g. (presumably) the
execution of Charles I; the defeat of King James II at the
Battle of the Boyne). This was diluted a little in the final Act,
where the offence is now composed of 'a statement that is
likely to be understood by some or all of the members of the
public to whom it is published as a direct or indirect encour-
agement or other inducement to them to the commission,
preparation or instigation of acts of terrorism'.[18] Other provisions cover the dissemination of terrorist material and
various 'precursor crimes' – i.e. conduct that might be leading
up to but does not itself constitute terrorist conduct.[19] The
legislation has produced a steady rate of convictions, about
23 per year from 2006 to 2009 (albeit none in 2009–10).[20]

Whether there are or are not convictions, the chilling
effect of these provisions (together with similar offences in
the Terrorism Act 2000) has almost certainly been substantial. Occasional glimpses of their breadth emerge from the
case law. There is the well-known incident at Nottingham
University where a lecturer was suspended after writing a
critical report on how two men had been arrested on terrorism charges when the research work of one of them (involving the downloading of an Al-Qaida training manual) came
to the attention of the authorities.[21] In *R v Gul*,[22] the appel-
lant was a law student at Queen Mary College who had been
arrested and charged under s 2 of the Terrorism Act 2006
for having uploaded videos onto the internet 'which the
Crown contended encouraged the commission of terrorism

as defined in section 1 of the Terrorism Act 2000 (as amended). Included in the videos were scenes showing attacks on soldiers of the Coalition forces in Iraq and Afghanistan by insurgents.'[23] After one deadlocked trial, the second jury sought guidance as to why military action against coalition forces in Iraq had to be deemed terrorism. It wondered too whether the use of force by British and American troops could ever be deemed terrorist. The trial judge helped as much as he could, saying (correctly) that 'the use of force by Coalition forces is not terrorism. They do enjoy combatant immunity, they are ordered there by our government and the American government, unless they commit crimes such as torture or war crimes'.[24]

Gul was convicted and sentenced to five years in jail, less time spent in remand, a decision that was upheld by the Court of Appeal with brutal clarity: 'The definition in s 1 [of the Terrorism Act 2000] is clear. Those who attacked the military forces of a government or the Coalition forces in Afghanistan or Iraq with the requisite intention set out in the Act are terrorists.'[25] As for the sentence, admittedly 'at the upper end of the range':

> The videos were in part glorifying and encouraging attacks on the forces of Her Majesty then serving in Iraq and Afghanistan. The seriousness of such conduct has to be marked by significant sentences of imprisonment despite the youth of the appellant and the serious consequences this conviction will have for the rest of his life.[26]

On 11 November 2011 the British Home Secretary banned a Moslem group (Muslims against Crusades) under the 2000 Act after it was judged that their conduct (which in the previous year had involved disrupting Remembrance Day events and the burning of poppies) amounted to the glorification of terrorism. The association had planned a 'Hell for Heroes' protest during the upcoming weekend.[27] Earlier that year, five Moslem men who verbally disrupted a homecoming march by soldiers in Luton in 2009 had their convictions for public order offences upheld by the Administrative Court.[28]

The district judge had said that she had no doubt that it was 'abusive and insulting to tell soldiers to "Go to hell" – to call soldiers murderers, rapists and baby killers' and that it was 'not just insulting to the soldiers but to the citizens of Luton who were out on the streets that day to honour and welcome soldiers home.' Citizens of Luton were 'entitled to demonstrate their support for the troops without experiencing insults and abuse'.[29]

Of course we can easily assert that the views challenged in these cases were unacceptable, beyond the pale of ordinary political discourse. But this is to betray our own assumptions about right and wrong, rooted in who we are and what we believe liberty to entail. For many in Britain (and of course further afield) British military action abroad, with the deaths and the proven inhuman and degrading treatment of local people that it entails, is a moral disgrace. As such for some it is perceived as imposing an obligation of resistance. The *Gul*, Nottingham, 'Muslims against Crusades' and Luton cases make clear that whatever about their show of universal application, these kinds of offences have usually only one target in mind – the radical speech of those outside the mainstream, the vulnerable few whose liberty of speech is easily sacrificed at an altar of security, a security which now sees risk not only in what people do but in what they say and think as well. Things are invariably quite different where it is a 'mainstream' English protest. So when the right-wing English Defence League were planning an inflammatory march in the Summer of 2011, the Communities Secretary Eric Pickles defended his initial decision not to act by asserting that 'English values of tolerance' were just too 'precious' to 'snuff them out by suppressing others'. Where this group was concerned, the whole issue had become an 'immensely difficult balancing act'.[30] It was much the same in the 1930s when the government and police were very reluctant to tackle Fascist demonstrations while being more than willing to break up Communist Party agitation.[31]

Nor does that other well-established democracy the United States, with its much vaunted free speech guarantee, provide much protection – again, just as it also failed to do in earlier security scares.[32] In *Holder v Humanitarian Law Project*,[33] the First Amendment proved itself incapable of protecting an association which was prevented by law from advising groups designated as 'foreign terrorist organizations' by US law. It was irrelevant that the assistance being offered related only to manifestly non-violent activities since, as the Chief Justice John Roberts put it, '[s]uch support frees up other resources within the organization that may be put to violent ends'.[34] Speaking for three dissentients, Justice Stephen Breyer asserted that '[n]ot even the "serious and deadly problem" of international terrorism can require *automatic* forfeiture of First Amendment rights'.[35] The banned groups include the Kurdish organization the PKK and Palestine's Hamas, the sorts of people, in other words, distant from the American mind when it directs its collective attention to the celebration of that tradition of liberty from which so much of its confidence flows.

Even that law pales by comparison with that signed into law by President Obama on 31 December 2011. This is a new provision of the National Defence Authorization Act for 2012 which purports to permit indefinite detention for all those (including American citizens) who can be shown to have 'substantially supported' Al-Qaida, the Taliban or associated forces, 'including any person who has . . . directly supported such hostilities in aid of such enemy forces'.[36] Having been challenged by a group of writers and political activists concerned about its breadth, this vague provision has already begun its long journey to possible resolution in the Supreme Court where, of course, *Humanitarian Law Project v Holder* will be an important authority in favour of its preservation.[37]

Seen against a background of such coercive anti-speech laws, invariably aimed at political opinions outside the mainstream, it can hardly be a surprise to find that newer, less-established democracies, have also followed suit. There is the young woman who has been detained for over four months for having displayed a banner objecting to a missile shield programme in Turkey, or as the law under which she is to be tried puts it 'making propaganda for a terrorist organization.'[38] There are also forty journalists in Turkey whom we have already briefly encountered in Chapter 4, arrested for suspected links with a banned Kurdish organization.[39] In Ethiopia a long-running trial continued through Spring 2012 with the 24 defendants involved including political activists and journalists charged with supporting a political party designated terrorist by the government.[40] The proceedings were brought under a 2009 anti-terrorism law which specifically clamps down on 'terrorist' speech and whose frequent use has already led to a strongly critical collective statement from no fewer than three independent UN human rights experts.[41]

In Yemen a journalist Abdul Ilah Haydar Shae is on hunger strike in prison, having been detained in August 2012 and subsequently imprisoned for 'participating in an armed band and having links with Al-Qaida'.[42] His crime appears to have been that he secured an interview for *Al-Jazeera* with the radical cleric Anwar al-Awlaki, himself subsequently killed by American forces.[43] In Burundi, a reporter for *Bonesha FM* and the Swahili service of *Radio France Internationale* Hassan Ruvakuki was detained 'in an abduction-style arrest' at the end of 2011, and subsequently charged with participating in acts of terrorism through collaboration with a rebel group. It appears that his arrest may have been prompted by *Bonesha FM*'s broadcasting of an interview with a man identifying himself as the commander of a new rebel group in the east of the country, the FRD-Abanyagi-hugu.[44] In Uganda Amnesty International has published a report, *Stifling Dissent: Restrictions on the Rights to Freedom of Expression and Peaceful Assembly in Uganda*, detailing the extent to which, among other coercive laws, anti-terrorism powers are being used to close off legitimate political debate.[45] On 19 August 2011, a court in Kazakhstan ordered a block on 13 foreign internet websites, including the popular LiveJournal Russian blog platform, on the grounds that they 'spread materials with propaganda of terrorism and religious extremism and open calls to committing acts of terror and making explosive devices'.[46]

So far as there is a repressive dimension to this, all that the CTC can say, when detailing the extent of worldwide movement under the protective umbrella of Resolution 1624 that has occurred, is to refer to the concerns of other institutions within the UN and lament the difficulties it faces in this field:

> However, international human rights bodies and others have also raised the concern that certain measures aimed at tackling incitement may have been excessive or overreaching and may have infringed on human rights, including the rights to freedom of expression and freedom from discrimination. This could be counterproductive, as it creates the risk that certain communities may become alienated from national and international counter-terrorism efforts. Implementation of resolution 1624 (2005) is especially challenging owing to the different definitions given by States to incitement and to the term terrorism itself.[47]

## A New Front Against the Different

There are many similar examples of the repressive deployment of domestic laws (whether or not expressly under the aegis of resolution 1624) laid out with gloomy authority on a monthly basis by the bulletin on counter-terrorism and human rights, issued by the International Commission of Jurists.[48] The move against religion in Kazakhstan just mentioned is an ominous sign as to what these security clampdowns on speech can often entail – a direct assault on the religious liberty that is so vital to the leading of full lives by so many people. Once again, if cover is needed, Resolution 1624 can be prayed in aid. Here is what the CTC's executive team has to say on the subject:

> In reviewing States' submissions on their implementation of the resolution, the Executive Directorate noted that relatively little attention was paid to the provision calling upon States

to 'prevent the subversion of educational, cultural, and religious institutions by terrorists *and their supporters*' (para. 3). There could be several reasons for this. Most fundamentally, any regulation touching upon such institutions is sensitive, since it would impact directly on such rights as those to freedom of access to information and ideas; cultural freedom; and freedom of thought conscience and religion. The development of regulatory frameworks in this area is thus challenging in a substantive sense and is further complicated in many States where there are limited human and financial resources available. There are added complexities where such institutions receive support from foreign States and entities. The Executive Directorate considers that this area deserves further study and action to achieve more effective implementation of the resolution.[49]

Kazakhstan's new law, ostensibly rooted in the need to tackle terrorism and religious extremism, requires re-registration of all religious communities, bans unregistered religious activities and introduces high penalties for violations of the ban. Religious organizations must submit to a 'religious study examination' by a government body, and there are restrictions on the distribution of religious literature outside of religious buildings, religious educational institutions and other facilities.[50]

Even Britain has published government papers recently, widening the net of the wrong kind of speech to catch nonviolent extremism and (sometimes) controversial speakers, with the yardstick of unacceptability being (it might be thought paradoxically) 'the vocal or active opposition to fundamental British values, including democracy, the rule of law, individual liberty and mutual respect and tolerance of different faiths and beliefs'.[51] France has its burqa ban[52] and Switzerland its clampdown on minarets[53] while a hardening of attitudes towards the different (immigrants, Moslems, gypsies) is being seen across Europe. The UN Special Rapporteur on Freedom of Religion and Belief, Heiner Bielefeldt, warned in March 2012 that 'state-sanctioned religions risk alienating minorities and discriminating against members of other faiths'.[54] Linked to this, it is hard to resist the conclusion as well that, as an earlier UN report put it, 'States have used the pretext of security in response to terrorist threats to limit the exercise of . . . the right to freedom of religion or belief.'[55] But as the British definition of extremism shows us, this goes beyond enmity to the religious other. Those of us fortunate enough to enjoy liberty in fact as well as in theory seem to see enemies everywhere and appear quite prepared to truncate their liberty while contriving to continue to believe not only in our own freedom but in liberty as a universal value. This is a neo-democratic self-deception that needs to be exploded. The starting point of such work is to insist on reconceptualizing security and it is with this I begin my next – and last – chapter.

# 7

# Returning to Universals

## Human Security

There is no need to accept the elision of security with state protection in the way that an exclusive preoccupation with terrorism seems to force us to do. The international community has long intuited the need to articulate a different vision of what it means to be safe, one that is more in keeping with the supranational idealism that provided the necessary[1] ethical impulse for the construction of the United Nations after the Second World War. The task is not dissimilar to that faced by the Levellers all those years ago in England,[2] albeit now on a larger scale: how do you construct a society in which all can get a decent chance to lead full lives, without an undue fear on the part of some (indeed many) of them that the misfortune of their particular situation means that it is impossible for them to get even the opportunity to do well?

Gerd Oberleitner has remarked that '[h]uman security has become a catchphrase in the global debate on the changing meaning of security'[3] and he is absolutely right that this idea has grown into the rallying slogan for human rights universalists in their struggle over meaning. The underlying reach of the term had been articulated before, albeit not in precisely this form, in large-scale reports such as those of the

Palme Commission in 1982,[4] the Brandt reports of 1980 and 1983,[5] the Brundtland Commission of 1988[6] and, after the end of the Cold War, the Commission on Global Governance of 1995.[7] The United Nations Development Programme (UNDP) produced a highly influential development report in 1994 which articulated policy in human security terms[8] and the Canadian government then enjoyed some success in developing the idea as a foreign policy initiative.[9] A human security network was created[10] and a strong commission chaired by Sadako Ogata and Amartya Sen published an influential report in 2003,[11] at which point the Secretary General of the UN was in the process of setting up an advisory board on human security[12] and a human security branch was being established in the UN's Vienna office on drugs and crime.

So what does this powerful term 'human security' mean? The Ogata and Sen Commission took as their starting point the idea that it extended 'to protect the vital core of all human lives in ways that enhance human freedoms and human fulfilment'.[13] The report's authors continued:

> Human security means protecting fundamental freedoms – freedoms that are the essence of life. It means protecting people from critical (severe) and pervasive (widespread) threats and situations. It means using processes that build on people's strengths and aspirations. It means creating political, social, environmental, economic, military and cultural systems that together give people the building blocks of survival, livelihood and dignity.[14]

Here we see how interconnected are liberty and security – the ideas that drive this book – when the second of these terms, security, is viewed in this broad, universalistic way. The Millennium Development Goals, agreed on 18 September 2000, demonstrate the link from the other angle, defining freedom as the right of men and women 'to live their lives and raise their children in dignity, free from hunger and from the fear of violence, oppression or injustice'.[15] This interconnectedness is even clearer in the following remarks by the then Secretary General of the UN Kofi Annan, which he made in the course of a workshop on human security as early as May 2000 (and which are quoted in the Ogata and Sen Commission):

> Human security in its broadest sense embraces far more than the absence of violent conflict. It encompasses human rights, good governance, access to education and health care and ensuring that each individual has opportunities and choices to fulfil his or her own potential. Every step in this direction is also a step towards reducing poverty, achieving economic growth and preventing conflict. Freedom from want, freedom from fear and the freedom of future generations to inherit a healthy natural environment – these are the interrelated building blocks of human, and therefore national, security.[16]

The last remark is of interest here, with its ambitious attempt to force the idea of national security into the more universalist (and therefore we would say, following the theme of this book, ethically effective) world of human security. Of equal interest but more dispiritingly however, is the date when these comments were made: some sixteen months before the attacks of 11 September 2001 brought with the reaction to them a renewed focus on the narrowest but most deeply rooted of all security paradigms and the one that I have been confronting throughout this book. This is the approach to 'security' which says that it is land that matters most and the people whose land it is whose security is all that counts.

Even without the events of 11 September, it is not likely that the vision of human security to which Annan, Ogata and Sen (as well as many others) subscribed would have been bound to have been successful. At very least it would have faced an uphill struggle seeking to counter the tendency towards neo-liberalism which, as we have seen, had already begun as early as the 1970s and which had spread across the world in the ten years after the end of the Cold War.[17] This promoted a market-based vision of the world, one which prioritized the freedom to trade over the well being of the population as a whole. To the extent that it had a moral dimension, then this was said to flow from the greater wealth that reached the poor via the effervescent commercial activities of the liberated traders.[18] Largely unproven even when asserted in its most ambitious form in its early 1980s heyday,[19] the sharp increases in inequality that it produced – and produce to this day[20] – were and are indisputable.

The great power of the *national* security discourse that has dominated the public mind since 2001 has been to divert attention away from rival understandings of security of the sort for which Annan, Ogata and Sen have been arguing. Clearly these would have placed such inequalities at the centre of the discussion, would have explained them as failings in human security and would then have demanded that something be done to alleviate them.[21] Of course occasionally this kind of activism does come off, the Make Poverty History campaign for example,[22] but even (undoubted) successes such as this – and other tangible advances in the realm of social and economic rights generally – can without cynicism be understood as a price capital willingly pays for that appearance of diversity that its protagonists judge (in an unconscious kind of way perhaps) to be in its best interests.[23]

## Fighting Denial

Throughout this book I have been discussing the way in which the powerful are able to persuade themselves to believe that the liberty and security which they enjoy are universals available to all and not just (largely) the consequences of their own lucky birth situations (right time; right gender; right country; right class). Hobbes began this for the embattled King of England and his privileged friends in the mid seventeenth century and it has carried on right into the era of the mass franchise. With the democratic hegemony that has followed the end of the Cold War, it has been recruited into a larger and equally vital narrative, one that stresses how – despite appearances to the contrary – we really do live in a world of equality, of freedom for all and respect for universal human rights. If neo-democracy were to be summed up in a single phrase, it would be collective self-deception.[24]

How can the alternative vision of liberty and security to which this book commits itself be realized in practice? The first thing to observe is that it is better to live in a world of double standards than in one in which it is not thought necessary to mask cruelty and inequality; hypocrisy is a route to critique which can in turn be managed into a passageway for change. Ideas like 'humanitarian intervention' and the 'responsibility to protect' – offshoots of the human security doctrine – can be made to do good work in the search for universal liberty and security just as they must be exposed as bogus when deployed to buttress rather than to reduce insecurity, by underpinning an invasion for example.[25]

Achieving this alternative conception of liberty and security raises further challenges. Much depends on the health of the underlying democratic culture, of how strongly embedded are the ideas of community solidarity and equality within any given political community itself. It may be that after the decades of deregulation and market hegemony that eventually led to the catastrophic market collapses of 2008, it is just possible that we may be seeing a slow recalibration of the political back into the sort of social democratic shape which has a better chance of taming the markets – and so pulling off the difficult feat of neither succumbing to their ethic nor at the same time giving in to the communist Nirvana which for so long and so distractedly was thought to be the their only alternative. If this is the case, and as I say it is by no means certain, then it might be that democracy will prove not merely to be the means to universal liberty and security in the future but rather to liberty and security for all, now. For this to be the case however democracies everywhere need to shed the inequalities that all such societies have inherited and which, as we discussed in Chapter 2, have long held back their progress in terms of realizing the kind of vision of security for which this book has been arguing. This is as true of places like Britain which have emerged (or indeed, as some might say, are still emerging) from aristocratic and landed rule into democratic freedom as it is of newer states unchaining themselves from centuries of colonial oppression.

To deliver universal liberty and security, democracy cannot do without a strong rule of law and an effective system of human rights protection. The first of these is about having a cohort of independent specialists, confident in their culture and knowledgeable of their field who are able and willing to take to their hearts the universalism inherent in the idea of law and then to apply it, without fear or favour. I am thinking here, above all, about the importance of an independent judiciary. Something like this kind of energy for integrity has driven the extraordinary resistance of Pakistan's legal profession to the political attacks on their chief justice which were so evident over many years at the end of the last decade.[26] It explains, too, the impressive ways in which some judges in the common law world have done their best (albeit, inevitably, only on those rare occasions when the accident of litigation have given them the chance) to hold democratic government to account for the equality to which it says it is committed.[27] Of course judges take wrong turnings and in some extreme cases are captured by vested interests,[28] but here is a resource that those truly committed to universal liberty and security should be loath to give up – an independent basis for that deep commitment to equality upon which a just society of any design must ultimately depend.

The same is true of human rights. Whether judicially enforced or not is a sideline issue here – this will depend on the specifics of the particular society under discussion. The key requirement is for human rights to act as a check against the drift to partisanship (i.e. selective liberty) to which (as we have seen) all democracies are vulnerable. Viewed in conservative terms, it is this engagement with human rights that protects a society committed to democracy from spilling over into a populist radicalism that would destroy altogether the activities of the market or (even) the very processes of democracy themselves. And there is a progressive perspective as well, one to the fore in much of what I have been saying in this book. With the egalitarian instincts of democracy being gradually superseded by the camouflaged selectivity of neo-democracy, the universalist assumption of human rights becomes an increasingly vital defensive shield through which to hold society to account for what, increasingly, it merely pretends to believe. Of course we have already seen how neo-democracies play at human rights, having this or that inspector in or receiving an adverse court ruling with apparent equanimity while all the time pushing its own exclusivist priorities. But human rights still have the power to force a way through this veneer and to uncover the selectivity underneath. We have seen many examples of just this process in this book, just as we have seen court rulings that have fought the same tendency.

## Liberty and Security for All

There is another reason why the rule of law and human rights are indispensable adjuncts to any democracy that is serious about retrieving the universality of its commitment to liberty and security which must stand as the ultimate test of its authenticity. This provides the answer to the national security question: 'how do you protect us?' Just as a society that has embraced a rich vision of what it means to be secure is not one that has given up on the markets, nor is it one that regards political violence – terrorism – as neither here nor there, a price worth paying for the grander liberty awarded to all. It is vital to stress that the protagonist of universal liberty is not some kind of anarchist libertarian, indifferent to the calamities wreaked by the untrammelled freedom of the few. Of course there are limits to liberty. The issue is not one of substance but of process: how do we work out *when* we should act against a person for the good of the whole community? And then, given we know we have to do something, *how* should we act? In particular how should we go about doing the necessarily coercive kinds of things that acting on our judgment will entail?

Finding the right answer to this question has been at the core of this book. I have been arguing that Hobbes gave us the wrong answer when he suggested (more or less) that we should hand it all over to Leviathan. But the Republicans too, for all their proto-democratic instincts, were equally in error in their determination to allow the state to defend itself *at all costs*. Of course democracies must defend themselves – but not at any price, and certainly not at one which so changes the shape of the society under threat that its survival has been achieved only at the price of its soul. Human rights and the rule of law return to guide us to the right way to tackle this dilemma, and their apparent old-fashioned qualities should not be mistaken for quaint irrelevancy.

Laws must be designed to prevent the sorts of destructive acts that threaten our security, and these offences should also embrace the planning, and preparation of such violence, as well as the incitement of others to do them. There may be other inchoate crimes that a society might need too, depending on circumstances. The key point though is in that word, 'crime'. It denotes the process through which all those suspected of such conduct are required to be put. And this is where human rights and the rule of law come back in. Before we punish, we must be sure. And to be sure we must be fair. The characterization of such wrongs as 'criminal' reminds us that this must be so and shows us too how we should go about ensuring such fairness: access to independent lawyers; a trial before an impartial tribunal (which in some cultures involves a lay jury); open justice; a presumption of innocence; careful rules of evidence to prevent abuse; an independent system of sentencing; and much else besides.

This is a system of protection for the state which achieves its goal through the protection of every individual as well. It is why neo-democracy with its special advocates, its secret proceedings, its administrative detention, its control orders and the like, desperately needs to unravel. Without such a system of open justice, a country is merely playing at democracy or, in the language of this book, has become a 'neo-democracy'. Properly understood and effectively deployed, human rights and the rule of law keep democracy honest, and all three together are the best chance we have of preserving the gains of past generations of democracy-makers for our children to enjoy. Not just our children, but every child – universal liberty and security.

# Notes

## 1  Introduction

1  J. Waldron, 'Security and Liberty: The Image of Balance' (2003), *Journal of Political Philosophy*, 11: 191, 195.

2  See for example, R. Clayton, H. Tomlinson, E. Buckett, and A. Davies, *Civil Actions Against the Police*, 3rd edn (London: Sweet and Maxwell, 2005).

3  See, for example, the remit for security adopted by the Institute of Public Policy Research, *Shared Destinies: Security in a Globalised World. The Interim Report of the IPPR Commission on National Security in the 21ˢᵗ Century* (London: IPPR, 2008).

4  There is a good account of the rise of the term in G. Oberleitner, 'Porcupines in Love: The Intricate Convergence of Human Security and Human Rights' in A. Melbourn and G. Gunner (eds), *Human Rights – From the Frontiers of Research* (Stockholm: Justus Förlag, 2005).

5  See the Beveridge Report, *Social Insurance and Allied Services*, Cmnd 6404 (November 1942), describing its vision as a 'Plan for Social Security' (para. 10).

6  E.g. those in Belfast, the US-Mexican border and the Indo-Bangladesh barrier. See the work of Niall Farrell on separation walls at http://www.marketplace.org/topics/economy/separation-barriers-world [last accessed 17 June 2012].

## 2  Struggling Towards the Universal

1  Now available to be read at http://www.earlymoderntexts. com/pdf/conslibe.pdf [last accessed 20 February 2012].

2  D. Miller, 'Introduction' in D. Miller (ed.), *Liberty* (Oxford: Oxford University Press, 1991), p. 6.

3  In what follows, I have been very influenced by the work of Quentin Skinner: see most recently his *Hobbes and Republican Liberty* (Cambridge: Cambridge University Press, 2008).

4  T. Hobbes. *The Elements of Law Natural and Politic* (1640, in F. Tonnies (ed.), 2nd edn, London: Simpkin, Marshall, and Co., 1889) (cited in Skinner).

5  n. 3 above, p. 36.

6  T. Hobbes, *Leviathan, The Matter, Forme and Power of a Common Wealth Ecclesiasticall and Civil* (1651, in R. Tuck (ed.), *Leviathan: Revised Student Edition*, Cambridge: Cambridge University Press, 1991), ch. 13, end of para. 9.

7  n. 3 above, p. 42. I think that Hobbes was right to think about human nature as fundamental, but wrong about how he saw human nature – but that is an entirely different book.

8  Hobbes, cited in Skinner, n. 3 above, p. 55.

9  Hobbes, n. 6 above.

10  Quoted in Skinner, n. 3 above, p. 126, n. 9.

11  M. Loughlin, 'The Constitutional Thought of the Levellers' (2007) 60 *Current Legal Problems* 1 at p. 1.

12  Accessible at http://www.constitution.org/lev/eng_lev_04.htm [last accessed 20 February 2012].

13  Loughlin n. 11 above, p. 8.

14  http://www.constitution.org/lev/eng_lev_04.htm [last accessed 20 February 2012].

15  Loughlin n. 11 above, p. 12.

16  Ibid. p. 20.

17  The document can be read at the web site of the Street Corner Society, 'dedicated to the memory of John Lilburne' at http://www.strecorsoc.org/docs/agreement.html [last accessed 29 May 2012].

18  T. Hobbes, *De Cive* (1642, Oxford: Clarendon Press, Eng tr., 1983).

19  Hobbes, cited in Skinner, n. 3 above, p. 151 n. 96.

20  E.g. T. M. Franck, 'The Emerging Right to Democratic Governance', *American Society of International Law* (1992), 86: 46.

21  Royal Commission on the Poor Laws and the Relief of Distress 1905–9. There is a good brief guide at www.fabians.org.uk/publications/extracts/brief-guide-horton [last accessed 20 February 2012].

22  See J. Kent, *William Temple: Church, State and Society in Britain 1880–1950* (Cambridge: Cambridge University Press, 1992).

23  http://docs.fdrlibrary.marist.edu/4free.html [last accessed 30 November 2009].

24  Skinner, n. 3 above, p. 154. See also Loughlin, n. 11 above. Of course the Levellers did not use today's language of economic and social rights but their goals were largely anticipatory of the contemporary human rights movement, albeit of course framed in a national rather than a global context.

25  The depressing data are at http://povertydata.worldbank.org/poverty/home/ [last accessed 28 May 2012].

26  Skinner, n. 3 above, p. 216. The very last sentence, immediately following this, is, 'But it is still worth asking if he won the argument'.

27  Apart from the continued exclusion of prisoners in a number of countries, including the UK, though the matter is currently under review in this jurisdiction, as required by the adverse Strasbourg ruling in *Hirst* v *United Kingdom (No 2)* [2005] 42 EHRR 849. (See further *Scoppola v Italy (no. 3)* (app 126/05, 22 May 2012.)

28  See J. Milton, *Areopagitica* (Speech to the Parliament of England, 1644).

29  Fascism has always been treated much more mildly: see so far as Britain is concerned K. D. Ewing and C. A. Gearty, *The Struggle for Civil Liberties* (Oxford: Oxford University Press, 2000), chs. 5 and 6.

30  'The safety of the people is the highest law': *Michaels v Block* (1918), 34 TLR 438.

31  *Liversidge v Anderson* [1942] AC 206.

32  *Thomas v Sawkins* [1935] 2 KB 249.

33  *Duncan v Jones* [1936] 1 KB 218.

34   As with the German Communist Party in the 1950s: see *German Communist Party Case* (1957) 1 *Yearbook of the European Convention on Human Rights* 222.

35   The best example among many being *Dennis v United States* 341 US 292 (1951).

36   Sir William Joynson-Hicks. The story is at K. D. Ewing and C. A. Gearty, n. 29 above, pp. 144–8.

37   [1765] 19 St Tr 1030.

38   E. P. Thompson, *Whigs and Hunters* (London: Allen Lane, 1975; Penguin edn, 1990), p. 267 (Penguin edn).

39   n. 36 above, 1066 (emphasis added).

40   A. V. Dicey, *Lectures Introductory to a Study of the Law of the Constitution*, 2nd edn (London: Macmillan, 1885). As my colleague Paul Kelly has pointed out to me, Bentham's strong critique of Hobbes was also in part responsible for the latter's revival in the nineteenth century.

41   Except insofar as they create space for democratic leaders to shift a little towards equality.

42   n. 40 above.

43   An example of his approach to one of these communities, the Irish nationalists, can be seen by perusing his brilliant polemic, *England's Case Against Home Rule* (1886), available from http://manybooks.net/authors/diceya.html [last accessed 30 November 2009].

44   The International Covenant on Social, Cultural and Economic Rights 1966.

45   The International Covenant on Civil and Political Rights 1966.

46   Greece brought great pressure to bear on the United Kingdom over Cyprus in the 1950s: see A. W. B. Simpson, *Human Rights and the End of Empire* (Oxford: Oxford University Press, 2001), ch. 18. And compare, albeit not strictly speaking a colonial situation, the *Ireland v United Kingdom* case (1978) 2 EHRR 25, arising out of allegations (afterwards substantiated) of the ill-treatment of internees.

47   *Whigs and Hunters* n. 38 above.

48   See generally M. Langford (ed.), *Social Rights Jurisprudence: Emerging Trends in International and Comparative Law* (Cambridge: Cambridge University Press, 2008) esp. Sandra Liebenberg (on South Africa, ch. 4) and Flavia Piovesan (on Brazil, ch. 9).

49 M. Mandel, 'A Brief History of the New Constitutionalism, or "How We Changed Everything so that Everything Would Remain the Same"', *Israel Law Review* (1998), 32, 250.

50 *Appleby v United Kingdom* (2003) 37 EHRR 783.

51 *Austin v United Kingdom* apps 39692/09, 40713/09, 41008/09 15 March 2012: http://www.bailii.org/eu/cases/ECHR/2012/459.html [last accessed 28 May 2012].

## 3   The Global Stage

1 UNSC Res 1368 (2001), paras. 1, 3, 4 and 5.

2 UNSC Res 1373 (2001), para. 3(a).

3 Ibid. para. 3(f).

4 Ibid. para. 6.

5 UNSC Res 1530 (2004). The other resolutions are UNSC Res 1438 (2002) (Bali); UNSC Res 1440 (2002) (Moscow); UNSC Res 1450 (2002) (Kenya); UNSC Res 1465 (2003) (Bogotá); and UNSC Res 1516 (2003) (Istanbul).

6 The details are in UNSC Res 1535 (2004).

7 UNSC Res 1611 (2005).

8 UNSC Res 1617 (2005). See below, pp. 46 for further details.

9 2178 UNTS 229, 9 December 1999.

10 n. 2 above, para. 3(d). The call had the required effect: the Convention came into force on 10 April 2002.

11 The full list of the relevant conventions is set out at an annex to the Convention, n. 9 above.

12 Ibid. art. 2.

13 Ibid.

14 E/CN.4/2006/98 (28 December 2005).

15 Ibid. para. 27.

16 Ibid.

17 UNSC Res 217.

18 UNSC Res 253 (1968).

19 UNSC Res 661 (1990).

20 See E. C. Luck, *UN Security Council: Practice and Promise* (Routledge: London, 2006) ch. 6.

21 UNSC Res 1333 (2000) para. 8(c).

22 UNSC Res 1363.

23 See UNSC Res 1390 (2002); UNSC Res 1455 (2003); and UNSC Res 1526 (2004) which added an Analytical Support and Sanctions Monitoring Team into the mix.

24 UNSC Res 1617 (2005). And see to similar effect UNSC Res 1735 (2006).

25 *United Nations Security Council and European Union Blacklists* Council of Europe Doc 11454 (16 November 2007) and its addendum dated 22 January 2008.

26 See G. Sullivan and B. Hayes, *Blacklisted: Targeted Sanctions, Preemptive Security and Fundamental Rights* (European Centre for Constitutional and Human Rights) pp. 61–3, the Treasury quote is at n. 166.

27 The full story is at *Blacklisted*, pp. 43–5.

28 http://www.911review.org [last accessed 19 August 2008]. The web site has since been reconfigured.

29 *Bosphorus Airways v Ireland* (2005) 42 EHRR 1.

30 Case T-315/01, *Yassin Abdullah Kadi v Council of European Union* [2005] ECR II- 3649; Case T-306/01, *Ahmed Ali Yusuf and Al Barakaat International Foundation v Council of European Union* [2005] ECR II-3353.

31 *Nada v Switzerland* 12 September 2012. Many of the EU cases are discussed in the *Blacklisted* report, n. 26 above.

32 New York, 2009.

33 Ibid. p. 3.

34 Ibid.

35 29 July 2005.

36 Ibid. para. 4.

37 Ibid. para. 5.

38 19 December 2006.

39 UNSC Res 1735 (22 December 2006).

40 30 June 2008.

41 Ibid. paras. 17–18.

42 Ibid. paras. 25 and 26.

43 17 December 2009.

44 Ibid. para. 20.

45 See her first annual report, Report of the Office of the Ombudsperson pursuant to Security Council Resolution 1904 (2009) (annex to S/2011/29) (accessible at http://www. securitycouncilreport.org/atf/cf/%7B65BFCF9B-6D27-4E9C-8CD3-CF6E4FF96FF9%7D/CT%201267%20S%20 2011%2029%20Ombudsperson%20First%20Report.pdf [last accessed 25 April 2012]. During the Summer of 2011 the mandate was extended for a further eighteen months: UNSC Res 1989 (17 June 2011) para. 21.

46  UNSC Res 1988 (17 June 2011) and UNSC Res 1989 (17 June 2011). Things are made worse for the Taliban suspects however as the procedures for the new list planned to cover them lack the full breadth of the safeguards now in place for the Al-Qaida cohort.

47  Statement by the Special Rapporteur on Human Rights and Counter Terrorism: see http://www.ohchr.org/en/NewsEvents/Pages/DisplayNews.aspx?NewsID=11191&LangID=E   [last accessed 26 April 2012].

## 4   The Enemy Within

1  Promotion and Protection of Human Rights E/CN 4/2006/98 (28 December 2005).

2  Ibid. para. 59.

3  Ibid. para. 60.

4  The details are at ibid. para. 60, notes 35 and 36.

5  See the BBC's country profile at http://news.bbc.co.uk/1/hi/world/europe/country_profiles/1102180.stm [last accessed 26 April 2012]. The US remark was from then Secretary of State Condoleezza Rice: http://news.bbc.co.uk/1/hi/world/europe/4467299.stm [last accessed 14 May 2012].

6  'UN Human Rights Panel Deplores Belarus Execution' UN News Centre 19 March 2012: http://www.un.org/apps/news/story.asp?NewsID=41581&Cr=Belarus&Cr1 [last accessed 1 May 2012].

7  'Tajikistan sentences 34 alleged Islamic terrorists' *Radio Free Europe; Radio Liberty* 19 April 2012: http://www.rferl.org/content/tajikistan_sentences_34_islamist_terrorists/24553622.html [last accessed 1 May 2012].

8  'Kazakhstan court jails 47 on terrorism charges after closed trial' *Washington Post* 19 April 2012: http://www.washingtonpost.com/world/asia_pacific/kazakhstan-court-jails-47-on-terrorism-charges-after-closed-trial/2012/04/19/gIQAnUYYST_story.html [last accessed 1 May 2012].

9  Emphasis added. Decision on Issues Related to Strengthening Anti-Terrorism Work: see http://www.loc.gov/lawweb/servlet/lloc_news?disp3_l205402874_text [last accessed 30 April 2012].

10   The original is at http://news.xinhuanet.com/politics/2011-10/29/c_111132865.htm [last accessed 30 April 2012].

11   US-China Joint Statement. The White House: Office of the Press Secretary: see http://www.whitehouse.gov/the-press-office/us-china-joint-statement [last accessed 30 April 2012].

12   'China amends Constitution to guarantee human rights' *Washington Post* 14 March 2004: http://www.washington post.com/ac2/wp-dyn?pagename=article&contentId= A57447-2004Mar14 [last accessed 30 April 2012].

13   In section 2 of the country's constitution – see http:// president.gov.by/en/press10669.html [last accessed 30 April 2012].

14   See http://president.gov.by/en/press10669.html [last accessed 1 May 2012].

15   As conceivably may be occurring in Burma: 'UN chief Ban Ki-moon meets Aung San Suu Kyi in Burma' BBC News Asia 1 May 2012: http://www.bbc.co.uk/news/world-asia-17904240 [last accessed 1 May 2012];

16   The constitution can be read at http://www.constitution.ru/ en/10003000-02.htm [last accessed 26 April 2012].

17   See the FCO report at http://www.fco.gov.uk/en/travel-and-living-abroad/travel-advice-by-country/country-profile/ europe/russia?profile=all [last accessed 27 April 2012].

18   Ibid.

19   Ibid.

20   For new laws restricting freedom of assembly promulgated in June 2012 see http://www.hrw.org/news/2012/06/08/russia-reject-restrictions-peaceful-assembly [last accessed 18 June 2012].

21   Comments of the Russian Federation on the Report by Commissioner for Human Rights of the Council of Europe, T. Hammarberg, following his visit to the Russian Federation from 12–22 May 2011 – accessible at https://wcd.coe.int/ ViewDoc.jsp?id=1851417&Site=CommDH&BackColorInter net=DBDCF2&BackColorIntranet=FDC864&BackColorLog ged=FDC864#Top [last accessed 27 April 2012].

22   The full transcript of the ABC News interview is at http://abcnews.go.com/2020/story?id=123996&page=1 [last accessed 27 April 2012].

23   Quoted in Report by Thomas Hammarberg, Commissioner for Human Rights of the Council of Europe, following his

visit to the Russian Federation from 12 to 21 May 2011 Comm DH 2011/21 6 September 2011.

24   S. Shuster, 'How the War on Terrorism Did Russia a Favor' *Time World* 19 September 2011 accessible at http://www.time.com/time/world/article/0,8599,2093529,00.html [last accessed 27 April 2012].

25   The whole law is to be found at http://www.coe.int/t/dlapil/codexter/Source/country_profiles/legislation/CT%20legislation%20-%20Russian%20Federation.pdf [last accessed 27 April 2012].

26   Male life expectancy in Russia hovers around the 60-year mark: http://www.google.co.uk/publicdata/explore?ds=d5bncppjof8f9_&met_y=sp_dyn_le00_in&idim=country:RUS&dl=en&hl=en&q=life+expectancy+in+russia#!ctype=l&strail=false&bcs=d&nselm=h&met_y=sp_dyn_le00_in&fdim_y=gender:1&scale_y=lin&ind_y=false&rdim=region&idim=country:RUS&ifdim=region&hl=en_US&dl=en&ind=false [last accessed 14 May 2012].

27   P. Preston, 'Putin's win is a hollow victory for a Russian free press' *The Observer* 11 March 2012: http://www.guardian.co.uk/media/2012/mar/11/putin-win-russian-free-press [last accessed 14 May 2012].

28   The various reports by the Commissioners, and Russia's responses, are usefully accessible at https://wcd.coe.int/search.jsp?ShowSectorBox=no&ShowSwitch=yes&ShowCrit=yes&ShowSectorLevelBox=no&ResultTitle=Click%20on%20'advanced%20search'%20for%20more%20criteria&ShowFileRefBox=no&ShowRes=yes&ShowFullTextSearch=yes&ShowPaginationBox=no&SearchMode=simple&Keyword=russian+federation+visit&Sector=secCommDH&CritTitle=none&Site=CommDH [last accessed 2 May 2012].

29   United Nations Human Rights. Office of the High Commissioner for Human Rights. 'Human rights chief calls for accountability on her mission to Russia' http://www.ohchr.org/EN/NewsEvents/Pages/HCMissionToRussia.aspx [last accessed 2 May 2012].

30   *Finogenov v Russia* 20 December 2011. A request to refer the case to the Court's Grand Chamber has been made.

31   *Edilova v Russia* 28 February 2012.

32   'Police arrest forty journalists on suspicion of Kurdish separatist links', *Reporters Without Borders* 20 December 2011:

http://en.rsf.org/turkey-police-arrest-25-journalists-on-20-12-2011,41578.html [last accessed 4 May 2012].

33 'Turkey: Arrests expose flawed justice system', Human Rights Watch 1 November 2011: http://www.hrw.org/news/2011/11/01/turkey-arrests-expose-flawed-justice-system [last accessed 8 May 2012]

34 The case can be accessed at http://actu.dalloz-etudiant.fr/fileadmin/actualites/pdfs/FEVRIER_2012/CASE_OF_FIDANCI_v._TURKEY.pdf [last accessed 4 May 2012].

35 See, e.g., *Ikincisoy v Turkey* 26144/95 European Court of Human Rights 15 December 2004.

36 *Izgi v Turkey* 15 November 2011.

37 For an overview of such activity see the web site of the UN High Commissioner for Human Rights: http://www.ohchr.org/EN/countries/ENACARegion/Pages/TRIndex.aspx [last visited 14 May 2012].

38 *The Definition of Terrorism* Cm 7052 (2007) table one.

39 'Malaysia: New ISA detentions show U-Turn on reform promises' *Amnesty International* 18 November 2011: http://www.amnesty.org/en/news/malaysia-new-isa-detentions-show-u-turn-reform-promises-2011-11-18 [last accessed 8 May 2012].

40 'Special rapporteur expresses concern about extrajudicial executions in India' United Nations Office at Geneva 30 March 2012: http://www.unog.ch/unog/website/news_media.nsf/(httpNewsByYear_en)/B04ACD8B61CBCB8EC12579D1004E13D7?OpenDocument [last accessed 8 May 2012].

41 Ibid.

42 *Stifling Dissent: Restrictions on the Rights to Freedom of Expression and Assembly in Uganda* Amnesty International: http://www.amnesty.org/en/library/asset/AFR59/016/2011/en/0d582c10-b11a-4119-bcde-13ec0d2718da/afr590162011en.pdf [last accessed 8 May 2012].

43 'Terror suspect found dead', *The Standard* (Kenya) 13 April 2012: http://www.standardmedia.co.ke/InsidePage.php?id=2000056177&cid=4& [last accessed 8 May 2012].

44 'Victoire Ingabire boycotts Rwanda terror trial' BBC News 17 April 2012: http://www.bbc.co.uk/news/world-africa-17739619 [last accessed 8 May 2012].

45 The three victims had disappeared sometime between 1994 and 1996 and had never reappeared. CCPR, Human Rights Committee, communication 1811/2008 (24 January 2012) *Djamel and Mourad Chihoub v Algeria*: http://www. ccprcentre.org/doc/OP1/Decisions/103/1811%202008%20 Chihoub%20v.%20Algeria_en.pdf [last accessed 8 May 2012]; CCPR, Human Rights Committee, communication 1781/2008 (18 January 2012) *Kamel Djebrouni v Algeria*: http://www.ccprcentre.org/doc/OP1/Decisions/103/1781%20 2008%20Djebrouni%20v.%20Algeria_en.pdf [last accessed 8 May 2012].

46 'Kenya sends troops to attack al-Shabab' *Al Jazeera* 24 October 2011: http://www.aljazeera.com/news/africa/2011/1 0/20111016115410991692.html [last accessed 8 May 2012].

47 As a result of SC Res 1535 (26 March 2004).

48 See the General Assembly resolution at A/Res/60/288 (20 September 2006): http://daccess-dds-ny.un.org/doc/UNDOC/ GEN/N05/504/88/PDF/N0550488.pdf?OpenElement [last accessed 10 May 2012].

49 Annex to ibid., 'Plan of Action' (emphasis added). See now the UN Global Counter-Terrorism Strategy: Activities of the United Nations System in Implementing the Strategy (April 2012).

50 Opening statement at the special meeting of the Counter-Terrorism Committee (28 September 2011): http://www.un. org/en/sc/ctc/docs/2011/2011-09-28-specialmtg-msmith.pdf [last accessed 12 May 2012].

51 Ibid.

52 http://www.un.org/sg/statements/?nid=5576 [last accessed 12 July 2012].

53 The full programme for the Symposium is at http://www. un.org/en/terrorism/ctitf/pdfs/chairman_summary_sg_ symposium.pdf [last accessed 9 May 2012].

54 n. 52 above.

55 http://www.un.org/en/sc/ctc/docs/2011/2011-09-28-specialmtg-puri.pdf [last accessed 9 May 2012].

56 Ibid.

57 n. 50 above.

58 See http://www.un.org/en/sc/ctc/docs/2011/2011-09-28-specialmtg-outcome.pdf [last accessed 9 May 2012].

59   S/2011/463: http://daccess-dds-ny.un.org/doc/UNDOC/GEN/
     N11/451/21/PDF/N1145121.pdf?OpenElement [last accessed
     10 May 2012].
60   The Ambassador's cover letter to the Secretary-General,
     ibid.
61   Ibid. Impact Survey para. 15.
62   Ibid. para. 18.
63   Ibid. para. 283.

## 5   A Very Partial Freedom

1   The whole speech can be read at http://www.bartleby.com/124/
    pres67.html [last accessed 15 May 2012].
2   On which see further ch. 6.
3   There is some interesting data and an effort at analysis at
    http://www.cbsnews.com/2100-500160_162-4728399.html
    [last accessed 15 May 2012].
4   'After the attacks: the overview; long battle seen' *New York
    Times* 16 September 2001: http://www.nytimes.com/2001/
    09/16/us/after-the-attacks-the-overview-long-battle-seen.
    html?pagewanted=all [last accessed 15 May 2012].
5   Roughly translated as 'let the good of the people be the
    supreme law' – see above p. 17.
6   The text is at http://www.gpo.gov/fdsys/pkg/PLAW-107publ40/
    html/PLAW-107publ40.htm [last accessed 16 May 2012].
7   The speech, delivered on 5 March 2012, is at http://www.
    justice.gov/iso/opa/ag/speeches/2012/ag-speech-1203051.
    html [last accessed 16 May 2012]. See further 'The Efficacy
    and Ethics of the President's Counterterrorism Strategy':
    speech by John O. Brennan, the Assistant to the President for
    Homeland Security and Counterterrorism, at the Woodrow
    Wilson Center 30 April 2012: http://www.wilsoncenter.org/
    event/the-efficacy-and-ethics-us-counterterrorism-strategy
    [last accessed 18 June 2012].
8   J. Risen and E. Lichtblau, 'Bush lets US spy on callers without
    courts', *New York Times*, 16 December 2005: http://www.
    nytimes.com/2005/12/16/politics/16program.html?page
    wanted=all [last accessed 16 May 2012].
9   See generally D. Cole and J. Lobel, *Less Safe, Less Free: Why
    America is Losing the War on Terror* (New York: New Press,
    2007).

10   The details are in K. Roach, *The 9/11 Effect: Comparative Counter-Terrorism* (Cambridge: Cambridge University Press, 2011), 187–188. This book is an excellent guide to the way that many established democracies reacted to the 11 September attacks.

11   And eventually acquitted of all charges brought against him: http://www.nytimes.com/2006/11/18/nyregion/18immigrant. html [last accessed 17 May 2012].

12   'FBI apologies to lawyer held in Madrid bombings': http://www.msnbc.msn.com/id/5053007/ns/us_news-security/t/fbi-apologizes-lawyer-held-madrid-bombings/ [last accessed 17 May 2012]. 'US will pay $2 million to lawyer wrongly jailed': http://www.nytimes.com/2006/11/30/us/30settle.html?_r=1&ref=brandonmayfield [last accessed 17 May 2012].

13   See section 802. The Act is accessible at http://www.gpo. gov/fdsys/pkg/PLAW-107publ56/pdf/PLAW-107publ56.pdf [last accessed 17 May 2012].

14   Roach n. 10 above, pp. 175–84 has the details.

15   s 2(a). For the whole order see http://www.fas.org/irp/offdocs/ eo/mo-111301.htm [last accessed 17 May 2012].

16   s 4(a).

17   s 7(b).

18   s 7(a).

19   Principally *Ex parte Quirin* 317 US 1 (1942) and also (from shortly after the war) *Johnson v Eisentrager* 339 US 763 (1950).

20   *Rumsfeld v Padilla* 542 US 426 (2004).

21   Ibid. p. 465.

22   He was eventually convicted: see http://news.bbc.co.uk/1/ hi/2037444.stm [last accessed 19 May 2012].

23   *Hamdi v Rumsfeld* 542 US 547 (2004).

24   The full text of the agreement between Hamdi and the US is at http://news.findlaw.com/wp/docs/hamdi/91704stlagrmnt. html and makes fascinating reading [last accessed 21 May 2012].

25   542 US 466 (2004). The vote was six to three with Scalia J. in the minority on this occasion.

26   Notably the Detainee Treatment Act 2002, followed by *Hamdan v Rumsfeld* 548 US 557 (2006).

27   Military Commissions Act 2006.

28  553 US 723 (2008).
29  Executive Order 13492 (22 January 2009). See http://www. whitehouse.gov/the_press_office/ClosureOfGuantanamo DetentionFacilities [last accessed 22 May 2012].
30  The report drawing this conclusion, dated 22 January 2010, can be accessed at http://cdm16064.contentdm.oclc.org/ cdm/singleitem/collection/p266901coll4/id/3111/rec/5 [last accessed 22 May 2012]. Forty-eight inmates fell into this category.
31  Executive Order 13567: http://www.gpo.gov/fdsys/pkg/ FR-2011-03-10/pdf/2011-5728.pdf [last accessed 22 May 2012].
32  s 1(b).
33  s 6.
34  s 3(a)(5).
35  Roach n. 10 above p. 211.
36  *Ireland v United Kingdom* (1978) 2 EHRR 25.
37  See p. 17 above and p. 96 below.
38  See http://news.bbc.co.uk/1/hi/uk_politics/7062237.stm [last accessed 23 May 2012].
39  Ibid.
40  Ibid.
41  *Brannigan and McBride v United Kingdom* (1993) 17 EHRR 539.
42  Human Rights Act s 3(1).
43  Anti-terrorism, Crime and Security Act 2001, s 21 (as originally enacted).
44  See Privy Counsellor Review Committee, *Anti-terrorism, Crime and Security Act 2001 Review Report* HC 100 18 December 2003 para. 183 for the details: accessible at http://www.statewatch.org/news/2003/dec/atcsReport.pdf [last accessed 23 May 2012].
45  The leading case being *Chahal v United Kingdom* (1996) 23 EHRR 413.
46  These two examples are, respectively, ss 57 and 56 of the Terrorism Act 2000.
47  For ten of them in a single ruling on 29 October 2003: see *Privy Counsellors' Review* para. 184.
48  See p. 5 above.
49  *A v Secretary of State for the Home Department* [2004] UKHL 56, [2005] 2 AC 68.

50 Prevention of Terrorism Act 2005.

51 *Secretary of State for the Home Department v AF, AE, AN* [2009] UKHL 28 at para. 81 per Lord Hope.

52 *Secretary of State for the Home Department v AH* [2008] EWHC 1018 (Admin).

53 *Secretary of State for the Home Department v AU* [2009] EWHC 49 (Admin).

54 *Secretary of State for the Home Department v GG* [2009] EWHC 142 (Admin).

55 *Secretary of State for the Home Department v AP* [2011] UKSC 24.

56 Terrorism Prevention and Investigation Measures Act 2011. And see also the Protection of Freedom Act 2012, reducing the ordinary limit on detention without charge in terrorism cases from 28 to 14 days, albeit with a power of extension in an emergency: see ss 57 and 58.

57 There is much useful information on the control order regime in D. Anderson, *Control Orders in 2011. Final Report of the Independent Reviewer on the Prevention of Terrorism Act 2005* (March 2012): http://www.statewatch.org/news/2012/mar/uk-terr-rev-control-orders-2011.pdf [last accessed 25 May 2012].

58 Roach n. 10 above p. 309.

59 Ibid. p. 310.

60 ASIO Legislation Amendment Act 2003.

61 'Anti-terror legislation in Australia and New Zealand' in V. V. Ramraj, M. Hor, K. Roach and G. Williams (eds), *Global Anti-terrorism Law and Policy* 2nd edn (Cambridge: Cambridge University Press), pp. 541–69, esp. 561–6.

62 Roach n. 10 above, 361–425.

63 Commission of Inquiry into the Actions of Canadian Officials in Relation to Maher Arar, *Report of the events relating to Maher Arar: Analysis and Recommendations* (Ottawa: Public Works and Government Services, 2006).

64 (2008) 30 (7) *London Review of Books* 3–8 (10 April).

65 'Businessman in US custody after losing extradition fight' *Guardian* 24 February 2012: http://www.guardian.co.uk/law/2012/feb/24/christopher-tappin-police-extradition-us [last accessed 25 May 2012].

66 The so called Nat West three: http://www.guardian.co.uk/business/blog/2012/mar/27/fraud-natwest-three-case [last accessed 18 June 2012].

## 6 Cultural War

1 See p. 17 above.
2 I explore this in more detail in my *Civil Liberties* (Oxford: Oxford University Press, 2007) ch. 3 ('Democratic Freedom and National Insecurity').
3 See p. 17 above.
4 K. D. Ewing and C. A. Gearty, *The Struggle for Civil Liberties* (Oxford: Oxford University Press, 2000) p. 147.
5 See p. 86 above; *R. (Brind) v Secretary of State for the Home Department* [1991] 2 AC 696. The Republic of Ireland also had a ban: *The State (Lynch) v Cooney* [1982] IR 337.
6 M. Ignatieff, *The Lesser Evil: Political Ethics in an Age of Terror* (Edinburgh: Edinburgh University Press, 2004).
7 W. Gutteridge (ed.), *The New Terrorism* (London: Mansell Publishers, 1986), p. ix.
8 28 September 2001. See chs. 3 and 4 above for discussion of the content and impact of this important resolution.
9 The full speech is at http://www.pbs.org/newshour/bb/international/jan-june99/blair_doctrine4-23.html [last accessed 3 June 2012].
10 The full speech is at http://www.guardian.co.uk/politics/2004/mar/05/iraq.iraq [last accessed 3 June 2012].
11 I. Cram, *Terror and the War on Dissent. Freedom of Expression in the Age of Al-Qaeda* (Dordrecht: Springer, 2009) 39, citing C. Walker, 'The Legal Definition of "Terrorism" in UK Law and Beyond' [2007] *Public Law* 331.
12 UNSC Res 1624 (14 September 2005) para. 1.
13 Ibid. paras. 5 and 6. We have already encountered this body: see p. 31 above.
14 Ibid. para. 4.
15 See p. 69–70 above.
16 CETS no 196, art 5. See Cram, n. 11 above, pp. 92–6 for further details.
17 A label Mr Blair always rejected: see his speech to the Foreign Policy Centre in March 2006, 'Not a Clash between

Civilisations, but a Clash about Civilisation': http://fpc.org.
uk/events/past/clash-about-civilisation [last accessed 3 June
2012].

18  Terrorism Act 2006 s 1. But note the idea of glorification still
    survives: ss 1(3) and 2(4).

19  The term is that of the Independent Reviewer of Terrorism
    Law, David Anderson QC: see his *Report of the Operation in
    2010 of the Terrorism Act 2000 and of Part 1 of the Terrorism
    Act 2006* (London: The Stationery Office, July 2011), para.
    10.5: http://terrorismlegislationreviewer.independent.gov.uk/
    publications/terrorism-act-2000?view=Binary [last accessed 3
    June 2012].

20  Ibid. paras. 10.23–10.24.

21  See the letter to the *Guardian* in defence of the lecturer
    (Dr Rod Thornton) where the background facts are concisely
    set out: http://www.guardian.co.uk/theguardian/2011/may/
    10/call-to-reinstate-terror-academci [last accessed 3 June
    2012].

22  [2012] EWCA Crim 280 (22 February 2012). The details in
    the text that follow are drawn from the judgment.

23  Ibid. para. 1.

24  Ibid. para. 11.

25  Ibid. para. 60.

26  Ibid. para. 75.

27  See http://www.channel4.com/news/theresa-may-bans-muslims-
    against-crusades-group [last accessed 6 June 2012].

28  *Munim Abdul v Director of Public Prosecutions* [2011]
    EWHC 247 (Admin).

29  See    http://news.bbc.co.uk/1/hi/england/beds/bucks/herts/
    8452616.stm [last accessed 6 June 2012]. Details of the failed
    appeal are at http://www.bbc.co.uk/news/uk-12480509 [last
    accessed 6 June 2012]. The Director of Public Prosecutions
    has now published guidance which seeks to adopt a consistent
    and principled approach to prosecutorial discretion in this
    area: http://www.bbc.co.uk/news/uk-17267271 [last accessed
    6 June 2012].

30  'EDL's online links with Norway killer fuel calls to ban
    London march', *Guardian* 29 July 2011 http://www.guardian.
    co.uk/uk/2011/jul/29/edl-norway-killer-london-march [last
    accessed 6 June 2012]. The planned march was eventually

banned by the Home Secretary after the Anders Breivik attack in Norway.

31 Ewing and Gearty, n. 4 above, ch. 6.
32 See above p. 17.
33 United States Supreme Court, 21 June 2010: see http://www. supremecourt.gov/opinions/09pdf/08-1498.pdf [last accessed 3 June 2012].
34 Ibid. p. 25 of the opinion of the Court (Roberts CJ).
35 Ibid. p. 5 of Justice Breyer's dissenting Opinion.
36 s 1021 of the Act.
37 See M. Hamblett, 'Ruling Blocks Aspect of Anti-Terror Detention Law', *New York Law Journal* 17 May 2012: see http://www.newyorklawjournal.com/PubArticleNY.jsp?id=1202554151792&slreturn=1 [last accessed 5 June 2012]. The full ruling is at http://www.nysd.uscourts.gov/cases/show.php?db=special&id=174 [last accessed 5 June 2012].
38 For further information see http://wwwi.bianet.org/english/human-rights/138260-banner-case-at-the-parliament [last accessed 5 June 2012].
39 'Police Arrest 40 Journalists on Suspicion of Kurdish Separatist Links' *Reporters Without Borders* 20 and 26 December 2011: http://en.rsf.org/turkey-police-arrest-25-journalists-on-20-12-2011,41578.html [last accessed 5 June 2012]. See also above p. 63.
40 Voice of America, 'Ethiopian Terrorism Trial Hears Voice of Defendant' http://www.voanews.com/content/ethiopian-terrorism-trial-hears-journalist-defendant-144654675/179445.html [last accessed 5 June 2012].
41 'Ethiopia's Anti-Terrorism Laws Must Not Be Misused to Curb Rights' UN News Centre 2 February 2012: http://www.un.org/apps/news/story.asp?NewsID=41112&Cr=journalist&Cr1= [last accessed 5 June 2012].
42 'Detained Journalist on Hunger Strike to Press for Release' *Reporters Without Borders* 15 February 2012: http://en.rsf.org/yemen-detained-journalist-announces-15-02-2012,41884.html [last accessed 5 June 2012].
43 See p. 76.
44 'Detained Radio Reporter to Face Terrorism Charges' *Reporters Without Borders* 2 December 2011: http://en.rsf.org/burundi-intelligence-agency-arrests-radio-29-11-2011,41481.html [last accessed 5 June 2012].

45 The Report, published in 2011, can be read at: http://www. amnesty.org/en/library/asset/AFR59/016/2011/en/0d582c10-b11a-4119-bcde-13ec0d2718da/afr590162011en.pdf [last accessed 5 June 2012].

46 'Mounting Concern About Kazakhstan's Use of Cyber-Censorship' *Reporters Without Borders* 26 August 2011: http://en.rsf.org/kazakhstan-mounting-concern-about-kazakhstan-26-08-2011,40858.html [last accessed 5 June 2012].

47 Global Survey of the Implementation by Member States of Security Council Resolution 1624 (2005) S/12/16 (9 January 2012) para. 14: see http://www.un.org/ga/search/view_doc. asp?symbol=S/2012/16 [last accessed 7 June 2012].

48 See http://www.icj.org/default.asp?nodeID=401&langage=1 &myPage=E-Bulletin_on_Counter-terrorism_and_Human_ Rights [last accessed 5 June 2012].

49 n. 47 above para. 100 (emphasis added).

50 'OSCE human rights chief expresses concern over restrictions in Kazakhstan's new religion law': http://www.osce.org/ odihr/83191 [last accessed 6 June 2012]. The law came into force on 13 October 2011.

51 *CONTEST The United Kingdom's strategy for countering terrorism* (Cm 8123 July 2011) and *PREVENT STRATEGY* (Cm 8092 June 2011). The definition quoted in the text comes from *Prevent*, annex A 'Glossary of terms'. For a critique see my 'Is Attacking Multi-Culturalism a Way of Tackling Racism, or Feeding it? Reflections on the Government's *Prevent* Strategy' [2012] (2) *European Human Rights Law Review* 121.

52 'France's Burqa Ban: 'Women Are Effectively under House Arrest', *Guardian* 19 September 2011: http://www.guardian. co.uk/world/2011/sep/19/battle-for-the-burqa [last accessed 7 June 2012].

53 'Swiss Ban on Minarets Draws Widespread Condemnation', *Guardian* 30 November 2009: http://www.guardian.co.uk/ world/2009/nov/30/switzerland-ban-minarets-reaction-islam [last accessed 7 June 2012].

54 UN News Centre, '"State Religions" risk alienating Minorities, warns UN Rights Expert': http://www.un.org/apps/news/ story.asp?NewsID=41468&Cr=religion&Cr1= [last accessed 6 June 2012].

55 Elimination of all Forms of Religious Intolerance. Interim Report by Abdelfattah Amor, Special Rapporteur of the Commission on Human Rights on Freedom of Religion or Belief, A/58/296 (19 August 2003): http://daccess-dds-ny.un. org/doc/UNDOC/GEN/N03/472/58/PDF/N0347258.pdf? OpenElement [last accessed 6 June 2012]. The quote in the text is at para. 139.

# 7 Returning to Universals

1 Though of course not sufficient: political necessity was also an inevitable driver of the change and influenced the precise construction of the UN more than did its idealist architects. See S. Moyn, *The Last Utopia: Human Rights in History* (Cambridge, MA: Harvard University Press, 2010).
2 See p. 10 above.
3 G. Oberleitner, 'Human Security – A Challenge to International Law?' (2005) 11 *Global Governance* 185, at 185.
4 Independent Commission on Disarmament and Security Issues, *Common Security: A Blueprint for Survival* [The Palme Report] (New York: Simon and Schuster, 1982).
5 W. Brandt et al., *North-South: A Program for Survival* (Cambridge: MIT Press, 1980) (see http://www.stwr.org/special-features/the-brandt-report.html [last accessed 8 June 2012]) and W. Brandt et al., *Common Crisis: North-South Cooperation for World Recovery* (Cambridge: MIT Press, 1983).
6 The World Commission for the Environment and Development, *Our Common Future* UN GA A/42/467 annex: http://www. un-documents.net/wced-ocf.htm [last accessed 8 June 2012].
7 Commission on Global Governance, *Our Global Neighbourhood* (Oxford: Oxford University Press, 1995).
8 UNDP, *Human Development Report 1994: New Dimensions of Human Security* accessible at http://hdr.undp.org/en/ reports/global/hdr1994/ [last accessed 8 June 2012].
9 There is much useful information at http://www.human security.info/ [last accessed 8 June 2012].
10 See http://www.hpcrresearch.org/research/human-security-network [last accessed 8 June 2012].
11 Commission on Human Security, *Human Security Now* (New York: Commission on Human Security, 2003): http://www.

policyinnovations.org/ideas/policy_library/data/01077/_res/
id=sa_File1/ [last accessed 8 June 2012].

12 See http://ochaonline.un.org/OutreachandABHS/tabid/2128/
language/en-US/Default.aspx [last accessed 8 June 2012].

13 n. 11 above, p. 4.

14 Ibid.

15 United Nations Millennium Declaration A/RES/55/2 (18
September 2000): http://www.un.org/millennium/declaration/
ares552e.pdf [last accessed 15 June 2012].

16 n. 11 above, p. 4.

17 See above p. 28.

18 For an update on this idea see N. Timmins, 'OECD calls time
on trickle-down theory' *Financial Times* 5 December 2011:
http://www.ft.com/cms/s/0/fba05442-1f3e-11e1-ab49-00144
feabdc0.html#axzz1xSashnlH [last accessed 10 June 2012].

19 See the famous remarks of David Stockman when President
Ronald Reagan's budget director in the early 1980s, when he
admitted that the theory was just some new clothes for the
unpopular doctrine of the old Republican orthodoxy of
cutting taxes: W. Greider, 'The Education of David Stockman'
*Atlantic Monthly* December 1981: http://www.theatlantic.
com/magazine/archive/1981/12/the-education-of-david-stock-
man/5760/1/ [last accessed 10 June 2012].

20 OECD report 'Divided We Stand: Why Inequality Keeps
Rising (December 2011): http://www.oecd.org/document/51/
0,3746,en_2649_33933_49147827_1_1_1_1,00.html     [last
accessed 10 June 2012].

21 Emblematic is the name given to the group set up by the
Institute of Public Policy Research in the UK to consider
'security in a globalized world': it was called the Commission
on National Security in the 21st Century. See its interim report
*Shared Destinies* (London: IPPR, 2008).

22 See http://www.makepovertyhistory.org/whatwewant/debt.
shtml [last accessed 15 June 2012].

23 See I. Manokha, *The Political Economy of Human Rights
Enforcement* (Basingstoke: Palgrave Macmillan, 2008).
Perhaps the Millennium Development Goals, n. 15 above, fit
into this analysis as well?

24 Or states of denial: see S. Cohen, *States of Denial: Knowing
about Atrocities and Suffering* (Cambridge: Polity, 2001).

25  Oberleitner n. 3 above has details on the interconnectedness between these terms.

26  See International Bar Association, *The Struggle to Maintain an Independent Judiciary: A Report on the Attempt to Remove the Chief Justice of Pakistan* (July 2007); International Bar Association, *A Long March to Justice. A Report on the Independence of the Judiciary in Pakistan and Related Matters* (September 2009): http://www.ibanet.org/Human_Rights_Institute/Work_by_regions/Asia_Pacific/Pakistan.aspx [last visited 12 June 2012].

27  For a good illustration of a British example of this, see T. Bingham, *The Rule of Law* (London: Allen Lane, 2010).

28  The US Supreme Court being a good general example almost since its establishment. But even at least a few of the conservative members of that court drew the line at some of the worst excesses of President Bush's 'war on terror': see pp. 81–3 above.

# Index

Abu Ghraib prison 79, 83
*Achille Lauro* hijacking (1985)
  75
Afghanistan 36
  UN sanctions against
    Taliban 37–8
Afghanistan war 75
Africa
  use of anti-terrorism laws to
    stifle dissent 65–6
*Agreement of the People,
  An* 10
al-Awlaki, Anwar 76, 79, 104
Al Barakaat International
    Foundation of
    Sweden 42–4
Al Taqwa Islamic Investment
    Bank 38–9
Al-Qaeda 30, 31, 37, 47, 80,
  88
Algeria 66
Amnesty International 65
  *Stifling Dissent* report 104
Angola 37
Annan, Kofi 110
anti-speech laws 9, 25, 98,
  99–105, 106

Anti-terrorism, Crime and
    Security Act (2001) 88–91
assassinations, 'targeted' 75–6
Australia
  anti-terrorist legislation 93
authoritarianism 11, 33, 35,
  36, 55
Awadallah, Osama 77, 79

Bagram Theater Internment
    Facility 79
Bali atrocities (2002) 31
Ban Ki-moon 67, 68
Belarus 51–2, 53–4
Belmarsh prison 89
Berlin Wall, collapse of 14
Bielefeldt, Heiner 106–7
bin Laden, Osama 31, 42,
  76
blacklists 38–49, 66
  challenging of by European
    courts 40, 41
  creation of Office of the
    Ombudsperson to help in
    delisting 47
  Kadi and Al Barakaat
    case 41–4, 47

blacklists (*cont'd*)
Nada case 38–9, 40, 41, 44, 122
PMOI case 40–1
UN reforms of 45–7
Blair, Tony 87, 88, 98, 100
Bogotá, terrorist attacks (2003) 31
*Bonesha FM* 104
*Boumediene v Bush* 82–3
Brandt reports 109
Brazil 24
Breyer, Justice Stephen 103
Britain 11, 12, 85–94, 106
Anti-terrorism, Crime and Security Act (2001) 88–9
detentions under 2001 Act 88–9
detentions under 2001 Act ruled as breach of right to liberty 90–1
Human Rights Act (1998) 87, 88
Muslims in 94
new system of control orders 91–2
shift in conventional thinking on liberty 86–7
Terrorism Prevention and Investigation Measures (TPIMs) 92
*see also* Northern Ireland
Brown, Gordon 86
Brundtland Commission (1988) 109
Burundi 104
Bush, George W. (and administration) 72–3
creation of detention camps 79

eavesdropping programme 76, 79
enforcement of immigration law 77
and Guantánamo Bay 80
and invasion of Afghanistan 75
and Patriot Act 79
response to September 11th 74–5
second inaugural address 72–3, 80
use of material witness warrants 77
'war on terror' 75, 76

Camden, Lord 18
Canada 109
anti-terrorist legislation 93
capitalism 27, 55
Carlile, Lord 65
CFI (Court of First Instance) 42, 43–4
Charles I, King 9, 11
Charles II, King 11
Chechnya 57, 58
Chihoub, Djamel and Mourad 66
China
definition of terrorism 52
and human rights 53
joint statement with US over counter-terrorism 53
civil liberties 1
civil rights 25
Cold War 74, 96
Commission on Global Governance (1995) 109
communism/communists 8, 17, 25, 96, 102
Constant, Benjamin 7

control orders (Britain) 91–2
Convention on the Prevention
   of Terrorism (2005)
   99–100
Council of Europe 38, 56, 99
counter-terrorism 2, 70
   and Bush administration *see*
      Bush, George W.
   and human rights 66–8, 70
   seizure of by some states as
      a weapon against internal
      dissent 51–4, 58–66, 69
   UN's agenda for 30–1, 32,
      33–6, 50, 55
   *see also* blacklists
Counter-Terrorism Committee
   *see* CTC
Counter-Terrorism Committee
   Executive Directorate *see*
   CTED
Counter-Terrorism
   Implementation Task
   Force 67
Court of First Instance *see* CFI
crime 115
CTC (Counter-Terrorism
   Committee) 31, 33, 50,
   51, 99, 105
   and human rights 51, 66–7,
      69–70, 71, 99
   reports on its impact in
      member states 69–70
   *see also* CTED
CTED (Counter-Terrorism
   Committee Executive
   Directorate) 31, 33, 66–7,
   70

Darling, Mr Justice 17
Declaration of the Rights and
   Duties of Man 23

democracy 4, 13, 16, 54–5,
   95, 112
   closing gap between culture
      and structure 54–5
   difficulties in transition to
      55
   representative 55, 95
   reshaping of by
      republicanism as 15
   resistance to egalitarian
      implications of 28
   transition to 19–20, 55
   *see also* neo-democracy
democratic turn 5, 26, 54
   imperfect success of and
      weaknesses 14–15
democratization 11
Dicey, Albert Venn 19, 21
Djebrouni, Kamel 66
double standards 112
Dubrovka theatre hostage-
   taking (2002) 61

eavesdropping programme 76,
   79
Edilov, Abdula 62
English civil wars 7
English Defence League 102
*Entick v Carrington* (1765) 18
equality 16, 20, 24–5, 28,
   112, 113, *see also*
   inequality
Ersanli, Büsra 63
ETA 31
Ethiopia 104
EU (European Union)
   blacklists established by
      40–1
European Convention on
   Human Rights 23, 25, 56,
   63, 87

European Court of Human Rights 39, 42, 57, 61–2, 64, 86, 87
European Court of Justice (ECJ) 43–4

Fabians 16
Federal Law No 35-FZ (Russia) 58–60
Fídanci, Mehmet 64
First World War 17
Foreign Intelligence Surveillance Act (FISA) (1978) 78
Foreign Office 57
franchise 11, 19

General Assembly (UN) 33, 34
Georgia 62
German Communist Party 25
Germany 12
Gil-Robles, Álvaro 61
Global Legal Monitor 52, 53
Greeks, ancient 7
Guantánamo Bay 75, 80–1, 82, 83–4, 89
Gul 100–1

habeas corpus 82, 83, 84
Haiti 36, 37
Hamas 103
Hamdi, Yaser 81, 82, 85
Hammarberg, Thomas 58, 61
Hawala banking system 42
Haydar Shai, Abdul Ilah 104
Heyns, Christof 65
Hizbullah 64
Hobbes, Thomas 63, 73, 115
    *De Cive* 10
    *Elements of Law* 8, 9
    *Leviathan* 9, 10, 22

theory of liberty 7–11, 13, 18, 19, 21, 111
Holder, Eric 76
*Holder v Humanitarian Law Project* 103
human rights 5, 13, 22–6, 27, 29, 115
    as a check against drift to partisanship 113–14
    and counter-terrorism 66–8, 70
    and CTC 51, 66–7, 69–70, 71, 99
    institutionalization of 23
    and neo-democracy 114
    Russia 57, 60–2
    Turkey 63–4
    and UN 32, 66
    universalist assumption of 114
    *see also* European Convention of Human Rights; European Court of Human Rights
Human Rights Act (1998) (Britain) 87, 88
Human Rights Watch 63–4
human security 2, 108–11, 112
humanitarian intervention 112

immigration law
    Bush administration's enforcement of 77
India 65
inequality 4, 13, 26, 27, 29, 111, 112 *see also* equality
Ingabire, Victoire 66
International Commission of Jurists 105

International Convention for the Suppression of the Financing of Terrorism (1999) 33–5
internment (Northern Ireland) 86
IRA 87
Iran 40
Iranian revolution (1979) 97
Iraq 36, 37
Islam 97
Islamic-based terrorism 92, 98
Islamic extremism 52, 98
Israel 3
Istanbul, terrorist attacks (2003) 31

judiciary, independent 113

Kadi, Yassin Abdullah 41–4, 47
Kazakhstan 52, 53–4, 104, 106
KCK (Union of Kurdistan Communities) 63
Kenya 66
    terrorist attacks (2002) 31
Khomeini, Ayatollah 40, 97
Kosovo 98
Kurdistan Workers Party *see* PKK

law, rule of 13, 18–22, 27, 28, 29, 41, 113, 115
Levellers 10, 12, 23, 108
    *An Agreement of the People* 10
Leviathan 19, 21–2, 74, 75, 115
Liberia 36
libertarianism 19

liberty-disavowal 10–11
Libya, bombings of (1986) 75
Lincoln, Abraham 73
LiveJournal Russian blog 104
Lloyd George, David 19–20
Locke, John 18
London bombings (2005) 31, 98
Lukin, Vladimir 62

Machiavelli, Niccolò 7
Madrid bombings (2004) 31, 77
Maduro, Miguel Poiares 43
Make Poverty History campaign 111
Malaysia 65
Marty, Dick 38
material witness warrants 77
Mayfield, Brandon 77–8, 79, 94
Medvedev, Dmitry 58
Military Commissions Act (2009) 85
Millennium Development Goals 109
Milton, John 16
Moscow, hostage taking (2002) 31
Moslem Brotherhood 38
Mubarak, Hosni 39
multiculturalism 14
Muslims, in Britain 94
Muslims against Crusades 101

Nada, Youssef 38–9, 40, 41, 44, 122
National Council of Resistance of Iran 40
National Defence Authorization Act 103

national security 1–2
National Security Agency 76
neo-democracy 29, 46, 48, 50,
    60, 86, 92, 96–7, 114,
    115–16
  as collective
    self-deception 112
  and human rights 114
  and neo-liberalism 6
  terrorism as facilitator for
    transition to 55–6
  and United States 83–5
neo-democratic turn 4, 5–6,
    13, 55, 71
neo-liberalism 6, 20, 28,
    110–11
New Deal 28
New Zealand, anti-terrorist
    legislation 93
9/11 *see* September 11<sup>th</sup>
    (2001)
Nixon, Richard 28
Northern Ireland
  broadcasting ban 86, 96
  and internment 86
Nottingham University 100

Obama, Barack 53, 75–6,
    83–4, 89, 103
Oberleitner, Gerd 108
Ocalan, Abdullah 64
Office of the Ombudsperson
    47
Ogata, Sadako 109, 110
Organization for Security and
    Co-operation (OSCE) 57

Padilla, Jose 77, 79, 80–2, 85
Pakistan 113
Palme Commission (1982)
    109

Patriot Act 78–9, 81
People's Budget 19–20
People's Mojahadeen
    Organization of Iran *see*
    PMOI
Periodic Review Board 84
Pickles, Eric 102
Pierce, Gareth 94
Pillay, Navi 61, 62, 68
PKK (Kurdistan Workers
    Party) 63, 64, 103
PMOI (People's Mojahadeen
    Organization of Iran)
    40–1, 42
political freedom 23, 33
political rights 23, 25, 56
poor laws 12
poverty 13, 29, 55, 110, 111
property rights 18–19, 25
Prost, Kimberley 47
pseudo-democracies 6, 41, 54,
    55, 57, 60, 61
Puri, Hardeep Singh 67, 69
Putin, Vladimir 57, 58

*R v Gul* 100–1
radicalism 4, 10, 16, 17, 25,
    28, 96, 113–14
*Radio France Internationale*
    104
*Rasul v Bush* 82
Reagan, President 28
religion 105–6
representative democracy 55,
    95
republicanism 9–10, 11–12,
    13–17, 26, 115
Roach, Kent 85
  *The 9/11 Effect* 77
Roberts, Chief Justice John
    103

Roosevelt, President Franklin
12, 23, 28
Rushdie, Salman 97
Russia 56–60
Chechnya wars 58
constitution and rights 56
engagement with external
criticism 57–8
and Federal Law No
35-FZ 58–60
human rights 57, 60–2
use of counter-terrorism as
weapon against dissent
57–61
Ruvakuku, Hassan 104
Rwanda 36, 66

*salus populi suprema lex* 17,
25, 75, 78, 85
sanctions, use of by UN 36–7
Scalia, Antonin 82
Scheinin, Martin 35–6, 47, 48
Second World War 23
Security Council *see* UN
Security Council
Sen, Amarya 109, 110
September 11th (2001) 29,
30, 35, 38, 55, 72, 87–8,
110
Bush's response to 74–5
UN's response to 97–8
Shanghai Cooperation
Organization 60
Sheinin, Martin 51
Skinner, Quentin
*Hobbes and Republican
Liberty* 8, 13
Smith, Mike 67, 69
social security 2
socialism 28
Somalia 66

South Africa 24
South America 27
speech, freedom of 17, 95,
102 *see also* anti-speech
laws
Stevens, John Paul 82
Sudan 36
Supreme Court 81, 82

Tajikistan 52, 53–4
Taliban 31, 37–8
Temple, Archbishop William
12
terrorism 14, 30–1, 33–4, 50,
68, 69, 114
China's definition of 52
fear of as facilitator of
transition to
neo-democracy 55–6
*see also* counter-terrorism
Terrorism Act (2000) (Britain)
87, 100, 101
Terrorism Act (2006) (Britain)
100
Terrorism Prevention and
Investigation Measures
(TPIMs) 92
Terrorism Suppression Act
(2002) (New Zealand)
93
Thatcher, Margaret 28
Thompson, E.P. 18, 24
Turkey 63–4, 104
Turkish Assembly of the Union
of Kurdistan
Communities 63

Uganda 65–6, 104
UN (United Nations) 32–3,
108
blacklists 38–40, 45, 46

UN (United Nations) (*cont'd*)
  counter-terrorism agenda
    30–1, 32, 33–6, 50, 55
  Global Counter-Terrorist
    Strategy (2006) 67
  goals of 32
  and human rights 32, 66
  response to September
    11th 97–8
  use of sanctions 36–7
UN Charter 30, 32
UN Development Programme
  (UNDP) 109
UN Human Rights
  Committee 66
UN Office on Drugs and
  Crime
  *Handbook on Criminal
  Justice Responses to
  Terrorism* 45
UN Security Council 30–1,
  32–3, 35, 45
  Resolution 1267 37
  Resolution 1373 30–1, 33,
    40, 50, 51, 53, 78, 97–8
  Resolution 1617 46
  Resolution 1624 98–9, 100,
    105
  Resolution 1730 46

Resolution 1822 46–7
Resolution 1904 47
Union of Kurdistan
  Communities (KCK) 63
United Nations *see* UN
United States 12, 19, 28,
  72–85
  and neo-democracy 83–5
  *see also* Bush, George W.
Universal Declaration of
  Human Rights 23
universal liberty and security
  11, 17–18, 27, 36, 41, 46,
  53, 57, 71, 83, 112–13,
  114–16

Waldron, Jeremy 1
war on terror 75, 80, 82–3
wealth disparities 13
Webb, Beatrice and Sydney 12
welfare state 12
Williams, George 93

Yemen 104
Yoo, John 76
Yugoslavia, former 36, 37

Zarakolu, Ragip 63
Zimbabwe 36